Tax Shelters

The Bottom Line

Tax Shelters

The Bottom Line

Robert A. Stanger

PUBLISHER
Robert A. Stanger & Company
Fair Haven, New Jersey

Published by Robert A. Stanger & Company
623 River Road, Fair Haven, New Jersey 07701

Copyright © 1982 by Robert A. Stanger.
All rights reserved. No portion of this book may
be used or reproduced in any manner whatsoever
without written permission from the publisher.
Printed in the United States of America
Library of Congress Catalog Card Number: 82-60132
ISBN 0-943570-01-8

ABOUT THE AUTHOR

Robert A. Stanger has spent his twenty-one year business career in the investment field, specializing for the past eleven years in tax shelter investments. While serving as First Vice President at White, Weld & Co. in the corporate finance department, he arranged both debt and equity financings for a wide range of commercial and multi-family residential properties. Over his career, other activities included public offerings and private placements in the fields of oil and gas exploration, cattle feeding and breeding, cable television and real property net leasing. Following the merger of his firm, Mr. Stanger became Vice President and Manager of the Merrill Lynch Tax Incentive Investment Department.

Mr. Stanger is a 1961 graduate of Princeton University with a B.A. in economics. He is a member of the Financial Analysts Federation, the National Leased Housing Association, the Real Estate Securities and Syndication Institute, and the New Jersey Chapter of the International Association of Financial Planners. He is a Registered Investment Adviser and a licensed real estate salesman in both N.Y. and N.J. He has been quoted frequently in the Wall Street Journal, Barrons, Forbes, Business Week, Newsweek, the New York Times and in numerous other publications and television shows.

In 1978, Mr. Stanger founded Robert A. Stanger & Co., publisher of **The Stanger Report: A Guide to Tax Shelter Investing** and **The Stanger Register: Tax Shelter Profiles.** These monthly reports are widely circulated among tax accountants and lawyers, stockbrokers, financial planners and other financial intermediaries involved in counselling clients about tax shelter investments. Robert A. Stanger & Co. performs consulting services for brokerage firms, banks and insurance companies with respect to the economic feasibility of tax sheltered transactions. As a registered investment adviser, the company performs similar assignments for individual investors. In addition, the company provides investment banking and corporate finance services to companies in the real estate and oil and gas businesses.

ACKNOWLEDGEMENTS

Fortunately, I have been associated with a broad range of highly motivated, professional individuals over the years. The common denominator among them all was a desire to create viable, economic investments that met the varied interests of those involved, from the developer/promoter to the attorney and the investor. Each one played a part in forming my approach to and refining my knowledge of tax sheltered investments. And each increased my respect for that breed of entrepreneur who starts a business and sees it through to a successful conclusion. My gentle push in this direction came from my wife Susan. I hope she feels as positively about it now, after the tremendous expenditure of time and effort — some of it hers — required to launch this enterprise.

— Robert A. Stanger
August, 1982

CONTENTS

Foreword — xv

INVEST IN TAX SHELTERS

Today's Economic Climate — 3
    The Case for Oil and Gas — 4
    What to Look for in Real Estate — 6
    High Interest Rates — 7
    The Effect of Inflation — 8
    New Tax Law Affects Shelters Favorably — 8
    IRS - The Bark and the Bite — 9

Your "Suitability" for Tax Shelters — 13
    Discretionary Income and Cash Flow — 14
    Predictability of Income — 15
    Type of Income — 15
    Liquidity — 16
    Risk Threshold — 16
    Human Element — 17
    Planning and Study — 17

Building Net Worth with Tax Shelters — 19
    Drilling for Oil and Gas — 19
    Building Low and Moderate Income Housing — 22

Why Economic Value Counts In Tax Shelter Investing — 25

INVESTIGATING TAX SHELTERS

Due Diligence in Tax Shelter Investments — 31
    Oil and Gas — 33
    Real Estate — 35

Tax Shelter Turn-Off Checklist	39
Nine Points	39
Additional Advice	42
Common Mistakes in Tax Shelter Investing	43

OIL AND GAS TAX SHELTERS

Why You Should Drill for Oil and Gas	51
Price Outlook	52
The Impact of the Windfall Profit Tax	53
New Tax Act Improves Oil and Gas Investment Returns	55
Higher Returns	55
More At Risk	57
How to Select a Good Oil and Gas Program	59
The Past Record	59
Success Ratios and Cash Tables	60
Who's Paying the Bills	61
Diversify	62
Guidelines	63
Deal Structure Doesn't Count	67
Types of Deals Available	68
Returns to Expect from an Oil and Gas Investment	73

REAL ESTATE TAX SHELTERS

Real Estate's Unique Characteristic	79
The Benefits of Real Estate Ownership	83
The Income Statement	85
The Cash Flow Statement	86
Summary of Benefits	87

**Real Estate: Improved Tax Shelter
Under the New Tax Law**   91
    The New Rules   91
    The Results   95

Judging Value in Real Estate Private Placements   97
    The Calculation of Value   98
    The Calculation of Cash Flow   99
    In Perspective   100
    Another Way to Judge Value   102

Investing in Public Real Estate Partnerships   109
    Real Estate Risks   109
    The Right Investment for You   111
    Investor Costs   114
    Reasons National Real Estate Partnerships
        Are Good Investment Vehicles   115

Apartments as Investments   119
    Supply Factors   120
    Demand Factors   122
    The Outlook for Rent Levels   123
    Other Factors   125
    Publicly Registered Partnerships   126

Buy Income Properties Now   129
    Demand and Supply Factors   130

Net Leases   133
    Economic Benefits   137

**Impact of the New Tax Law on Subsidized
Housing, New Construction and Rehabilitation**   139
    Tax Changes   141
    Impact on Tax Savings and Rates of Return   142

**Sale of Older Subsidized Housing
Partnerships Advisable**   147

OTHER SHELTER INVESTMENTS

Venture Capital - R & D Partnerships   153
    Tax Aspects   154
    Advantages   155

Oil Income Funds   157
    Returns Available in Income Funds   158
    How to Evaluate Deal Structures   159
    Management   162

ERTA is No Bonanza for Equipment Leasing   165

Thoroughbred Horses   171
    Horses and Taxes   174

THE ECONOMIC RECOVERY TAX ACT OF 1981

ERTA Affects Tax Shelters Favorably   179
    Tax Brackets and Rates   179
    Depreciation and Investment Tax Credits   180
    Personal Property   180
    Real Property   182
    Investment Tax Credits   184
    Underpayment Penalties   185
    Real Estate and ERTA   185
    Oil & Gas and ERTA   187
    Equipment Leasing and ERTA   187
    Commodity Straddles and ERTA   188
    Securities Dealers and ERTA   189
    R & D Shelters and ERTA   190

3 To 1 Write-Offs - Don't Try 'Em   191
    The Background   191
    The Change   193

EVALUATING RETURNS FOR TAX SHELTER INVESTMENTS

The Best Way to Compare Tax Shelter Investments	197
Return Calculations Made Easy	199
Calculating Internal Rate of Return	206
Comparing ARR to IRR	207
Alternative Methods	208
Other Factors	209
Rate-of-Return Calculation Worksheet and Instructions	211

SHELTER OUTLOOK

Tax Shelters - Alive and Well	219

1982 TAX LEGISLATION AND SHELTER INVESTMENTS

The Impact of 'TEFRA' on Tax Shelters	227
Abusive Shelters	229
Individual Minimum Tax	230
Index	233

FOREWORD

Each year inflation increases the basic price of income-producing assets and pushes more people into higher tax brackets. Direct ownership of hard assets through tax shelter investments can make you the beneficiary rather than the victim of rising prices. And, in addition to helping you profit from the cost spiral, tax shelter investments can cut your tax bill. As a result, in 1981, securities firms sold almost $8 billion of tax shelters to individuals.

This book provides our objective, unbiased views on two tax shelter investments to buy in the 1980's — real estate and oil and gas. We document the favorable economics for these investments and provide guidelines to help you make informed investment decisions. We believe that investors should pick tax shelter transactions based on investment merit, not just their potential tax benefits.

Most books on this subject help you to understand what tax shelters are. We assume you know what they are and have identified your need for them. Our intent is to show you what to look for and how to analyze particular transactions.

Much of the material contained in this book has been adapted from recent issues of **The Stanger Report: A Guide to Tax Shelter Investing.** This monthly report provides objective, unbiased information about tax shelter investments and the analytical tools required to make informed investment decisions.

INVEST IN TAX SHELTERS

TODAY'S ECONOMIC CLIMATE

In today's economic climate, some tax shelters make very good investment sense. Proper tax shelter investments enable you to put tax dollars to work to buy assets. Tax shelter investments are the only way to tap this source of cash and convert it directly to property that can increase your net worth substantially.

There's nothing illegal about investment tax shelters. You are using deductions provided by the tax code to reduce taxable income. These deductions are perfectly legitimate and are designed to encourage certain kinds of investments that generally benefit the economy.

The purpose of this book is to show you:

- which tax shelters make the most sense in today's economic climate,
- how they can impact your net worth, and
- how to select the best ones by concentrating on economic value, not just tax relief.

The climate for tax shelter investing is changing. The reasons behind the changes are complex, but basically they involve:

- soaring inflation,
- high interest rates,
- continuing escalation of basic energy costs,
- lack of new construction activity, and
- record numbers of people in high tax brackets, despite the tax relief provided by the Economic Recovery Tax Act of 1981.

The investments most enhanced by these developments are those which involve drilling for oil and gas and buying existing real estate mortgaged at yesterday's favorable rates. The investments most injured are new real estate construction ventures and transactions sensitive to short-term borrowing costs, such as transportation equipment leasing. To be sure, new real estate and equipment leasing deals aren't dead — it's just that they are less attractive, and good ones are harder to find.

Equally true, not all oil and gas transactions will benefit from these developments as the market is swiftly adjusting to the increased demand. In 1978, only 83 transactions were publicly registered. In 1979, there were 92; in 1980, 126; and in 1981 there were 193. Bad deals, those doomed from the first to produce poor results or those so structured to be heavily loaded against the limited partner, will be more plentiful than ever. So, the best advice is to be more careful now than ever before.

What about the "Windfall Profit Tax" that President Carter pulled out of Congress? It's adverse legislation — but there's little chance that it will have a dramatic negative impact on the search for new oil and gas reserves. The tax is higher on so-called "old oil" — oil drilled prior to the passage of the legislation. The lower tax on newly discovered oil doesn't hurt today's favorable economics for oil and gas drilling much at all.

Don't be alarmed by recent disclosures that world production is currently at or above demand. That situation is temporary. Within three to four years, the picture will change dramatically to one of scarcity. The reason: Reserves and production will continue to decline.

The Case for Oil and Gas

The case for oil and gas investment is compelling. These numbers tell the story: U.S. market prices for oil have risen 800% since 1973, from $4.25 per barrel to $32 or more. That compares with an increase in drilling costs of about 154%. Put the two together and it's not hard to see that the economics strongly favor the investor.

We now have crude oil price de-control. Or put another way, there's a free market for oil in the U.S. The price the industry paid for that freedom is the Windfall Profit Tax. The tax reduces profitability per barrel about 15% below prior levels. And, that's very little to suffer for an 800% price increase.

The case for natural gas is equally dramatic. The average price at the wellhead in interstate markets rose from 30 cents per Mcf (thousand cubic feet) in 1973 to 90 cents per Mcf in 1978 and to about $1.15 in 1979. These figures combine gas contracted at low prices years ago with newly discovered gas at much higher current prices. For instance, the controlled base price of new gas is now about $2.90 per Mcf while decontrolled natural gas sells for more than $8.50 per Mcf.

The following table shows average costs, reserves and values for gas wells in the United States:

Economics Of Drilling For Natural Gas

Year	Average Cost Per Gas Well	Reserves[1] Added Per Well	Price[2] Per Mcf	Value of Reserves Added Per Well	Ratio of Value To Cost
1973	$158,000	1.46	$ .40	$ 584,000	3.7
1974	155,000	1.22	1.00	1,220,000	7.9
1975	189,000	1.23	1.30	1,599,000	8.5
1976	262,000	.87	1.45	1,262,000	4.8
1977	270,800	.87	1.85	1,610,000	6.0
1978	314,000	.74	2.00	1,480,000	4.7
1979	367,000	.70	2.60	1,820,000	5.0
1980	451,000	.75	2.90	2,175,000	4.8

Source: Natural Gas Supply Association's Report on Natural Gas Supply and Demand.
(1) Millions of Mcf, or billions of cubic feet.
(2) Best estimate of intrastate gas prices per thousand cubic feet for new contracts after BTU adjustment, based on Department of Energy, "Monthly Energy Review".

As you can see, costs have risen 185% from 1973 to 1980. Reserves per well are only 51% of the level of seven years ago while prices have risen 625%. The net effect is to leave the ratio of value to cost intact, making gas wells a prime investment. And, notice the reserve value (at current prices) on average in 1980 is $2,175,000 compared to a well cost of $451,000.

Better yet, Amoco says that in their experience reserves discovered per foot of well drilled have not declined in twenty years. They should know. Amoco is the largest domestic driller, accounting for about 11% of all oil and gas exploration in the U.S.

What To Look For In Real Estate

High interest rates favor the purchase of existing properties over properties under construction. Newer properties can have a distinct competitive disadvantage relative to older properties in times of rapidly rising interest rates. The reason: The older property is probably financed with mortgage debt carrying far lower interest rates and debt service costs. Here is an example of a 200,000 square foot apartment building with an old mortgage of $3,850,000 at 9% interest and a 10.25% constant (the annual payment of interest and principal):

Rent	$840,000
Less:	
Operating Expenses & Taxes	-290,000
Cash Flow Before Debt Service	$550,000
Less:	
Debt Service	-395,000
Net Cash Flow	$155,000

Now change the debt service to an 11% interest rate and an 11.6% constant. The effect is dramatic:

Cash Flow Before Debt Service	$550,000
Less:	
Debt Service	-447,000
Net Cash Flow	$103,000

Changes in competitive or market factors could cause problems for either property. But, the property with the old mortgage can tolerate an 18% vacancy and still break even ($155,000 divided by $840,000). The same property with a new mortgage costing just slightly more can only stand a 12% vacancy and break even ($103,000 divided by $840,000). That's one advantage of lower-cost mortgage loans.

Alternatively, the older mortgaged property can suffer a 6% reduction in rents ($52,000 divided by $840,000) and still earn the same cash flow ($103,000) as the newly financed property fully rented.

High Interest Rates

High interest rates create additional problems for properties under construction because they can also increase building costs. Until the building is complete, construction is usually financed with a fluctuating rate loan over the bank prime lending rate. Larger buildings take eighteen months or so to build. With the prime rate at high levels, as it was in 1981, the added interest costs can mount up.

The harmful effect of high interest rates can also be seen dramatically in equipment leasing transactions. Transportation equipment (with the exception of aircraft which command higher lease rates than rail cars and barges) can only generate a gross lease rate (return before costs of ownership, operation and management) of possibly 15% on invoice cost.

However, if you borrow from a bank to buy and carry the equipment you usually pay the prime rate or higher. In addition, the total annual debt service costs can be quite a bit more than the interest charges alone because you are also repaying principal. So high interest rates on borrowing can eliminate your return.

When the cost of debt service exceeds cash flow from the property, you have "negative leverage." And, under these circumstances, your only real alternative is to repay the debt even though you are losing money. That's because you have to hold on to the equipment for five years in order to keep the investment tax credit, one of the major tax benefits of equipment leasing.

Yet, equipment leasing deals have been the fastest growing category of direct placement programs (tax shelters), according to the National Association of Securities Dealers. Expectations about inflation, and hence the future value of the property being financed, obviously outweigh carrying cost considerations for many investors.

The Effect of Inflation

A powerful argument can be made that direct ownership of physical assets can make you the prime beneficiary of inflation in the long term. Rising replacement costs have a positive impact on investment value. The reason: As the cost of new assets increases, the dollar return must also increase to maintain a fixed, competitive rate of return on investment.

Rising rents on new assets lead to an increase in rents on assets purchased at lower cost. And, if debt service carrying costs are fixed, the upside leverage can be great.

If, on the other hand, the return on new investment shrinks, construction or manufacture of new assets will decline. And, assuming continuing demand, pressure will exist to raise rents, and assets will sell at prices which are a function of their earnings. That's one way to translate inflation into profit.

New Tax Law Affects Shelters Favorably

Most tax shelters in the pipeline were snapped up before the ink dried on the Economic Recovery Tax Act of 1981 ("ERTA"). There were several reasons for the demand. Major tax rate reductions starting in 1982 put a premium on deferring income in 1981. Also, most investment-grade tax shelters supply larger benefits under the new law.

Surprisingly, deduction-oriented and income-generating shelters both benefit. Tax losses should increase because depreciation deductions are larger for equipment leasing and real estate. At the same time, the tax rate is lower on income from shelters that develop taxable income (oil and gas) or roll over taxable income (equipment leasing or cattle feeding). And all investments that develop economic value are enhanced by lower capital gains taxes.

In addition, the law creates lots of new tax benefits for buying existing real estate, making research and development expenditures and financing energy equipment.

The Big Losers under the law: commodities, futures and options straddles, securities dealer shelters and shelter schemes relying on "overvaluation" of assets for unrealistic depreciation deductions or investment tax credits.

IRS — The Bark And The Bite

Certain types of "exotic" tax shelters are being disallowed across the board by the IRS in audits of personal tax returns. On the other hand, most real estate and oil and gas deals are not provoking such activity. Further, audits are virtually unheard of for the big publicly registered tax shelters. That's the result of our survey of leading tax shelter specialists.

The IRS has announced and partially implemented a war against "abusive tax shelters." The IRS defines an abusive shelter as a promotion or scheme utilizing improper or extreme interpretation of tax law in order to obtain substantial tax benefits which are clearly disproportionate to their economic reality. In a few words, that's any "multiple write-off" deal (where tax loss substantially exceeds cash investment). Some of the steps taken are clearly unprecedented in scope and intensity. The real questions, though, are: How is the war being waged in practical terms? What's the IRS really after? How are they going about it? Can you learn enough about the system to benefit personally?

Get ready for the news — everyone agrees, the IRS approach is having a dramatic impact. The attack on abusive shelters is picking them off like flies. The types of deals most mentioned as IRS targets are book and record masters, lithographic plates, movies, T.V. programs, cattle, minerals, and investment and commodity straddles. The shelter issues identified broadly are recourse and non-recourse financing, inflated investment tax credits, inflated values, donations of property, large tax losses per dollar of investment, and loss-generating, but essentially riskless, transactions.

In fact, what's happening in these areas is just what the IRS says is happening — immediate disallowance of the claimed deduction, no negotiation with the Service, limited access to an appeal conference and an immediate invitation (30-day letter) to Tax Court.

Further, your odds of getting caught in Big Brother's net are increasing. For one thing, tax losses appearing on Schedules A, C, and F are being closely reviewed for "tax shelters" you own directly, not through a partnership. For another, many taxpayers are being pulled in when someone else in the shelter draws the Service's attention.

The IRS can now demand the names from the promoter or sponsor of all investors in the deal. In practice, that's exactly what's happening. The IRS pulls everyone's tax return and disallows everyone's deductions from the suspect transaction. In effect, the particular shelter is being disallowed.

Then, there's the new return audit selection criteria called TPI (total positive income). The effect of TPI is to put many tax shelter users in the one in nine audit probability category versus the current one in fifty category. No one has enough experience with the TPI approach to be able to judge its impact yet.

The overall partnership audit ratio is no higher than one in seven, or one in ten, in practice, and that's below the IRS objective of one in four. But, the overall record consists of many legitimate real estate and oil and gas partnerships and the publically registered deals that are hardly audited at all. The other component is "abusive shelters" which are taking a direct hit. Your odds of being nailed for this type of shelter are quite high.

Mind you, no one is saying the IRS interpretation of tax law is correct, but the IRS has issued many recent tax shelter pronouncements (called Revenue Rulings). The way the procedures stack up, the scorecard on the first skirmish reads IRS 1, taxpayers 0. That's because agents must refer certain tax shelter issues, the unpublished "hit list," to higher authority with no conversation, much less negotiation, with the taxpayer (unless you roll over and amend your return removing the questioned deduction). In the past, this step just set in motion an extended set of taxpayer delaying tactics. Often the taxpayer benefited because the interest rate on his tax deficiency was lower than market rates he could earn on the tax savings.

The IRS is trying to shorten the time period to settle tax deficiencies. The jury is still out on the actual impact. But new steps will help the IRS. Among them: lead tax shelter cases, consolidating cases, restricting access to the appellate process within the IRS, accelerating communication with taxpayers, and removing cases previously held in suspense and moving them to Tax Court.

Manpower shortages at the IRS and a congested Tax Court do auger well for the taxpayer. The IRS established return selection criteria so low that too many shelters qualify for audit. The resulting case load could be so high that the practical result may be IRS concentration almost solely on the obviously abusive tax shelters. Even here, the net catches the little fish along with the big ones which may also clog the wheels of justice.

Much lower audit activity occurs in "standard" real estate and oil and gas than in more exotic transactions. Almost no audit activity is reported for major publicly registered tax shelter partnerships. Activity in real estate transactions is lower than in any major tax shelter investment area.

STRATEGY NUMBER ONE: Avoid audit by staying with the big visible real estate, oil and gas and equipment leasing tax shelters. COROLLARY: Private placement investments in offbeat areas run an extremely high risk of audit and disallowance of deductions.

Theoretically, when your return is singled out, even if only for your tax shelter losses, the agent should look at your whole return. For high risk or aggressive returns this fact can spell danger. Don't be afraid of legitimate tax shelters or legitimate deductions. But, a combination of high risk tax shelters and other questionable deductions is ill-advised. Further, the IRS generally repeats your audit in subsequent years until you come up clean two years in a row. Once caught, forever harassed.

STRATEGY NUMBER TWO: At best, risky shelters only make sense when they're the only questionable items on your return. COROLLARY: Safe shelters and reasonable deductions on tax returns are as American as apple pie and are not the targets of recent IRS activity.

The IRS is educating agents to be much more aware of tax shelter issues. But, their awareness does not necessarily mean sophistication. What's happening is wholesale disallowance of all kinds of tax shelter deductions at the agent level (kicking the return upstairs if you will). Then, the legitimate tax shelter deductions usually make it through the supervisory level. Only the abusive ones don't survive. But, initially good and bad shelters are tarred with the same brush.

The burden of proof of investment intent and profit motive is on the taxpayer in tax proceedings. You are best advised to know the nature of the business in which you invest for tax shelter. The more esoteric the business, the more applicable the advice, and the more sophisticated you should be. The cost of legal defense in Tax Court is almost prohibitive. An estimate of minimum cost is $25,000. The more issues involved, the higher the cost. To fight the IRS is to pay anyway.

On the other hand, the Reagan Administration tax legislation for depreciation for both real property (buildings) and personal property (machinery and equipment) will help. One of the tremendous benefits of passage of this legislation is the elimination of uncertainty and taxpayer/IRS disagreements over the amount of depreciation you can take. The reason: The new rules are mandatory and are described as audit-proof. The IRS cannot take exception to that portion of your tax return if you follow the rules.

YOUR "SUITABILITY" FOR TAX SHELTERS

What makes an investor "suitable" for a tax shelter program? According to the SEC, the critical criteria are the investor's annual income and net worth (exclusive of home, furnishings and automobile). For instance, according to a regulatory standard for most public oil and gas programs, the investor must have either 1) net worth of $225,000, exclusive of personal possessions, or 2) net worth of $60,000 and taxable income of at least $60,000. (Some states impose even higher levels.)

In setting these somewhat arbitrary thresholds, the SEC may actually be doing investors a disservice. Taxable income is not nearly as important as other criteria such as discretionary income, predictability of income and type of income. And, net worth is an almost meaningless gauge of whether you are right for shelter. Your discretionary cash flow, liquidity position and personal risk threshold are far more important.

Your personality and attitude toward investing — in other words the "human" element — are important factors in determining "suitability." It's critical to determine how you feel about such things as illiquid investments, complicated documents and financing arrangements, and the possibility of wrestling with the IRS. Many tax shelters are an act of faith either in the business venture, or in the purveyor of the investment. That sinking feeling in the pit of your stomach may be too much to bear when the dude from Oklahoma rides into the sunset with your cash.

Furthermore, tax shelter investment decisions are all too often made one at a time, not with a view toward their overall impact on your net worth or the overall composition of your assets. Many professionals feel tax sheltering is most proper when executed in the context of total financial and estate planning requirements. Only the investor and his advisor can properly judge "suitability" in this perspective.

Matching a shelter's economic benefits with your needs requires balancing the expected results against those needs. Most tax shelters can only maximize one of the available benefits, either cash return, tax shelter or appreciation. Be realistic regarding the results you expect. Be sure the type of investment you make is designed to accomplish your objective. And remember emotional as well as financial "suitability" are a part of fulfilling your expectations.

In hindsight, of course, economically successful investments are suitable for almost anyone. But, assessing economic prospects and risks in shelters can be a tough job, especially for the layman. Risky ventures and extreme leverage are two causes of economic disaster. You should probably avoid them both. Very few investors understand (much less enjoy) having their investment wiped out, however large the tax benefits they accrue along the way.

Tax shelters are too often sold like "hot stocks." There's a pressured atmosphere to sign up and pay up. The tax and economic factors are not adequately explained nor the ramifications explored. Good shelters are hard to find, but about $8 billion worth of shelters were sold in total in 1981. In this rather large playground, there's a swing with your name on it. Relax. Take the time to study and be conscientious.

This, then, is our seven point checklist to help you determine your true "suitability" for tax shelters, beyond the legal requirements you must meet according to securities law.

1. Discretionary Income And Cash Flow

Most investment-grade shelters involve cash out-of-pocket — after spending tax dollars, you must still lay out your own cash. So you must be willing to draw down your capital to pay for a shelter, and your income after tax must be greater than your personal consumption expenditures. Many relatively high-income executives need tax shelter but don't have the discretionary income to make the investment because — as Parkinson's Law states — their expenses have risen to meet their income.

Some people borrow in order to buy tax shelters. The risk is that the shelter may go astray and/or there may be a call for more cash. A strained credit standing may not allow the necessary follow-on investment.

Some people cut salary withholding taxes to pay for their shelter investment. Tax shelter losses are now a legitimate reason for reducing the amount withheld from your paycheck. You may file a new W-4 to reflect your expected reduced tax bill from tax shelter losses, a good way to help with the cost.

2. Predictability Of Income

Many tax shelters possess investment and tax ramifications for many years; some don't. Match the shelters you select with your circumstances. Oil and gas deals generally create tax losses in the initial year of investment. Frequently, in the second year, you can be assessed (asked to make an additional investment). Some real estate net leases and subsidized housing transactions generate tax losses for eight or ten years.

Investors with widely fluctuating income (unless the income is always high and sometimes very high) are tough candidates for tax shelter planning. That's true not just because many shelters generate losses in later years, but worse, sometimes lots of income in one year. If high personal income and high shelter income periods coincide, the combined tax bite could be brutal.

As a general rule, tax shelter losses shouldn't reduce taxable income below $45,000 for a joint return ($35,000 single). This income level will be the 38% bracket in 1984. Reason: Tax shelters are usually priced to produce a reasonable return only for investors benefiting from tax savings at this rate or higher.

3. Type Of Income

If you are seeking to shelter capital gains or if you make very large charitable contributions, tax sheltering raises a special red flag. Because of the Alternative Minimum Tax created by the Revenue Act of 1978, tax shelter deductions may only benefit you to the extent of 20 cents on the dollar. This level of benefit would make tax shelter inappropriate and uneconomic.

Too much shelter may reduce the net tax benefit available. So-called "tax preference items" (such as intangible drilling costs on productive oil and gas wells and accelerated depreciation in equipment leases and real estate deals) are subject to a special add-on tax if you try to use too many deductions of this type.

4. Liquidity

Generally accepted wisdom suggests that you need "adequate" liquid, or marketable, investments before trying tax shelters. We subscribe to these conventional thoughts. Certainly, adequate life insurance and medical and disability coverage are priorities. And, liquid assets are necessary to cover contingencies (medical emergencies, a cash cushion to change jobs, etc.) But, high write-off tax shelters (equipment and real estate net leases) can build net worth almost entirely with tax savings. So one could argue there is good sense in pursuing these investments regardless of liquidity.

Older or retired investors must be sure estate tax obligations can be met, and often, tax shelters should be combined with insurance planning. Sometimes when shelters pass through estates, appreciation may escape taxes. Shelters like real estate result in a low tax basis for the original purchaser because of depreciation deductions. But, the "stepped-up basis" rules enable the heir to "mark the asset to market value" and establish a new tax basis, effectively eliminating tax on the appreciation.

5. Risk Threshold

Tax shelters involve tax, business and timing risks. So investors shouldn't press too hard to optimize results with shelters. Tolerances for loss and uncertainty vary, but one way to reduce risk is to diversify. Buying more than one kind of shelter and buying shelters over several years can be very sensible.

Often, investors with "suitable" financial capability and income characteristics don't need to maximize financial return. The combination of risk, leverage and complexity in shelters may not be appropriate if your only interest is preserving capital.

Finally, all shelters are more risky than you think. Probably the least risky are large diversified real estate syndications in which the portfolio consists of already built commercial property. Those with the most risk are leveraged shelters with no diversification in which all the economic value is expected to come from the exploitation of one asset.

6. Human Element

Tax shelter investing is different from buying stocks and bonds. Most of the time you can't kick and feel what you own, and you certainly can't look up the price in the paper. Tax shelter partnerships generally put out lots of reports and financial statements filled with strange words and concepts. Because of accounting practices, these statements often don't portray an accurate picture of the economic success or standing of the venture.

Understanding the significance and relevance of complex tax rules adds to the shelter buyer's job and complicates arriving at a "comfort level." Also, factors associated with shelters can increase the probability of IRS audit. Some people savour the challenge; some get chills at the thought.

Tax savings from shelters increase disposable income — and these tax savings are hardly ever "saved." But with many shelters, a tag should be placed on those dollars of tax savings identifying their rightful owner — Uncle Sam. Shelter buyers need the discipline to plan for and count on the tax ramifications of shelter ownership in future years — as well as the ability to enjoy the current tax benefits available under our system of taxation.

7. Planning And Study

You must analyze your income, net worth and asset composition on a multi-year basis to develop a proper tax shelter strategy. Here's why. The process will focus your attention on your ultimate objective of building net worth, introduce logic (versus emotion) in investment decisions, establish specific objectives, locate capital sources and lead to a plan of action.

Keep the process simple, but look ahead five years. Estimate your income, your deductions, your personal expenditures and any unusual financial requirements, like college tuition. Get some help from a professional to plug in the tax and economic consequences of different kinds of shelters. Create an overall shelter investment plan you can live with.

Now you can concentrate on selecting the kinds and amounts of investments to fit the plan. Implementation is the critical element. "Good" investments will create value.

The process of planning and study will acquaint you with your needs and with the benefits tax shelter investments can reasonably provide. You'll establish goals for tax sheltering that are realistic. Your expectations will be geared to likely results. You'll feel a lot more comfortable and be a much better client for your lawyer and your investment broker or advisor.

BUILDING NET WORTH WITH TAX SHELTERS

Let's assume you're one of the fortunate few who, after your personal expenses and tax payments, have some income left over that can be set aside each year for investment. If so, your personal income statement might look like this:

Personal Statement - A

Income	$100,000
Personal Deductions	-15,000
Exemptions	-5,000
Taxable Income	$80,000
Regular Tax Due*	$31,318
Income	$100,000
Tax Due	-31,318
Disposable Income	$68,682
Personal Expenses	-54,000
Available for Investment	$14,682

*1982 Federal Tax Rates.

Buying tax shelters can add substantially to your net worth because you'll be putting money to work for you which you would otherwise pay in taxes. The following two examples show how oil and gas and subsidized housing investments can increase your asset build-up. The results are dramatic.

Drilling for Oil and Gas

When you drill for oil and gas, you can deduct part of the cost immediately. The deduction consists of the so-called intangible drilling costs, or the amount you spend to drill the well to total depth. The rest of the cost is not immediately deductible. It is called the tangible drilling cost or the amount you spend to complete the well and equip the well to produce.

In many oil and gas drilling deals, the limited partner/investor only pays the intangible costs, so most of your investment may be immediately deductible. The general partner pays the tangible costs to earn his interest in the partnership.

It is normally possible to deduct up to 85% of the amount of the cost of this type of investment in the first year. A $25,000 oil and gas investment could generate $21,250 of deductions which will lower your taxes, as statement B shows.

Personal Statement - B

Income	$100,000
Oil & Gas Deduction	-21,250
Personal Deductions	-15,000
Exemptions	-5,000
Taxable Income	$58,750
Regular Tax Due	$20,693
Income	$100,000
Tax Due	-20,693
Disposable Income	$79,307
Personal Expenses	-54,000
Available For Investment	$25,307

Comparing Statements A and B, you'll notice a reduction of tax payments equal to $10,625. Add that to the amount available for investment shown in Statement A, $14,682, and you have $25,307 available for investment shown in Statement B.

That's 72% more money working for you with the oil and gas investment than without it.

Assuming the oil and gas investment is worth its cost after taxes, you've added $125,000 to your net worth over five years (if you put $25,000 a year into the oil and gas investment).

There are many ways to evaluate what your oil and gas investment might be worth. In general, its value will be determined by the amount of oil and gas reserves that are discovered and the time over which those reserves will be produced.

You realize the value of your oil and gas investment in one of three ways: Selling it back to the general partner in what's known as a liquidation offer; possibly exchanging it for stock; or by sticking with it and continuing to receive cash distributions.

A reasonable objective would be to attempt to find petroleum reserves that will produce future revenues of two times your cash investment. We feel that is an achievable objective especially if you diversify by making regular investments over a period of years. That means your $125,000 investment would generate approximately $250,000 of cash distributions to you over the average twelve-year life of the investment. (The cash distributions used in this example are accelerated two or three years from possible patterns in successful drilling programs.) Oil and gas reserves usually produce at a declining rate each year so that most of the income is received in the first five years. A typical pattern would result in $225,000 of cash distributions being received in the first ten years.

Cash Distributions

Year 1	$50,000	Year 6	$15,000
2	37,500	7	15,000
3	30,000	8	12,500
4	25,000	9	10,000
5	20,000	10	10,000

Most of these cash distributions are taxable, but about twenty-five percent of them would be tax free because of a deduction that's known as the depletion allowance. As an investment incentive, oil and gas income may be reduced by an artificial deduction, the depletion allowance, before taxes are calculated. In general, the impact is to lower tax rates for investors in the 50% tax brackets to only 37% on their oil and gas income.

The cash distributions above result in after-tax cash for the typical 50% investor as follows:

After-Tax Cash Distribution

Year 1	$31,500	Year 6	$9,450
2	23,625	7	9,450
3	18,900	8	7,875
4	15,750	9	6,300
5	12,600	10	6,300

Discounting these distributions at 6% results in a present value (after tax) of about $119,000, which is roughly equal to your cash investment of $125,000. So, an oil and gas program that results in reserve discovery equal to twice your investment is worth the investment on a present value basis after tax in addition to the tax savings the investment generates.

Building Low and Moderate Income Housing

Subsidized housing refers to various government programs that provide incentives for private investors to finance construction of apartments for individuals with low or moderate incomes. The most popular one today is the so-called "Section 8" program.

To oversimplify, in a Section 8 program the government pays the owner the difference between the amount of rent the tenants can afford and the total operating costs and debt service for the property. In return for this subsidy, the apartments must be rented to low or moderate income tenants for an extended period, usually 20 years or longer. As a result, you normally aren't free to sell the property, and this is the main drawback to a subsidized housing program.

Several special tax code provisions provide tax breaks for these investments. The deductions reduce your taxable income and hence save taxes. The result will be an increase in your net worth. Just like the oil and gas investment, it's funded by dollars which you would otherwise pay in taxes.

Let's assume you take the $14,500 you have available after all your expenses annually and make a subsidized housing investment in each of the next five years. And, let's assume you'll receive about 1.5 times your investment in deductions each year, a fairly typical relationship. Your investment would then generate $21,250 of deductions, and your personal financial statement would look like this:

Personal Statement - C

Income	$100,000
Sub-Housing Deduction	-21,250
Personal Deductions	-15,000
Exemptions	-5,000
Taxable Income	$58,750
Regular Tax Due	$20,693
Income	$100,000
Tax Due	-20,693
Disposable Income	$79,307
Personal Expenses	-54,000
Available For Investment	$25,307

But, you only put $14,500 of the amount available for investment into the subsidized housing tax shelter. That leaves $10,807 available for investment. After five years, you would have a portfolio of assets acquired at a cost of $54,035 and a subsidized housing investment of $72,500 ($14,500 times 5). Your net worth would be $126,535 with the shelter versus $73,410 if you just pay the tax.

But, what's the subsidized housing investment really worth? To the extent that inflation persists, the replacement cost of the apartment building you buy will probably be a lot higher. So, in terms of hard asset value, your investment might be worth a lot more than you paid for it. But remember, you're not free to get out from under your government subsidy contract. Therefore, let's take the worst case and assume that the property becomes run down, the neighborhood deteriorates, and you let the property go. The result is a foreclosure.

A foreclosure will obviously result in no cash to you. But, a foreclosure can create a taxable gain resulting in a capital gains tax which must be paid. Depreciation reduces your tax basis or cost. The amount of the foreclosed mortgage is considered the amount of the sale proceeds (explained in the next chapter, "Why Economic Value Counts in Tax Shelter Investing"). If the foreclosure takes place 17 years after your original investment when you have run out of depreciation, you could accumulate a sufficient reserve to pay the capital gains tax if you put aside your tax savings from the 11th year through the 17th year.

That means the tax savings from the year of the original investment through the tenth year are yours to keep even if the property is eventually foreclosed. These tax savings may constitute your entire return on investment. Usually the tax savings in the first five years will recover your capital outlay. So, the residual value of the subsidized housing investment will equal the present value of the tax savings from the sixth through the tenth years. In a typical example, the tax savings on a $72,500 subsidized housing investment would be:

Tax Savings

Year 6	$8,700
7	7,600
8	6,900
9	6,300
10	5,800
TOTAL	35,300

These tax savings equal $35,300 and constitute the real value of the investment even if the property is foreclosed. Remember you'll still have an investment portfolio at cost of $54,035. Your total net worth will increase by $89,335 (versus $73,410 with no tax shelter) even if the subsidized housing investment becomes worthless.

WHY ECONOMIC VALUE COUNTS IN TAX SHELTER INVESTING

The economic merit of any tax shelter and how it ultimately works out will affect its value to you. Obviously in the subsidized housing example in the previous chapter, if the investment had greater economic value, your net worth would have increased substantially more. Another factor comes into play when tax shelters die. If you dispose of a tax shelter, you can create taxable income whether or not you actually receive any cash. And, it doesn't matter whether you dispose of it by sale, gift or foreclosure (the lender takes the property).

So, if your tax shelter doesn't work out, you just can't forget it. The IRS won't let you, especially if you took tax losses greater than your cash outlay. And, you only receive tax losses larger than your cash outlay if the property is mortgaged or debt is involved. That's because you're allowed to include the amount of the debt in determining the cost of the property. Almost all tax shelter transactions rely on some amount of debt to maximize tax losses.

Being relieved of debt, even debt on which you're not personally liable (so-called non-recourse debt), confers a benefit on you — you don't have to repay it. The size of the benefit is equal to the amount of the debt. It is added to the proceeds of sale and enters the calculation of taxable gain. These rules apply to gifts and involuntary dispositions such as foreclosures, as well as the sale of the property.

Selecting tax shelters for their tax loss characteristics is one of the biggest mistakes investors make because there is usually a tax cost to dispose of tax shelter assets. Obviously, the greater the value of the asset, the more cash you will have to cover the cost of disposition. So, ultimately the real economic value of a shelter will determine whether it is a good investment.

How Debt is Figured In

If you buy property for $100,000 down and obtain a $900,000 mortgage, your cost as well as your tax basis for depreciating the property is $1 million. In this example, you are depreciating ten times your cash investment. So, the more debt the better, but that's true only up to a point.

The point is the time you dispose of the property either through sale or foreclosure. Your sale proceeds include the principal balance of the mortgage plus any cash you receive. Subtract your tax basis from the sale proceeds, and that's the amount of your gain for tax purposes.

Here's how it works. Let's assume you took $200,000 of depreciation on this property over several years, and that's the exact amount of the tax losses. Remember, you bought the property with $100,000 of cash and a $900,000 mortgage. Your tax basis is now $800,000. That's the original cost of $1 million, less tax losses of $200,000. If the property is not worth the mortgage and you let it go, sale proceeds equal the amount of the mortgage. You subtract your tax basis, and the balance is taxable income.

Sale Proceeds (Unpaid Mortgage)	$900,000
Tax Basis	-800,000
Taxable Income	$100,000

The transactions work out as follows: Net tax losses are $100,000 ($200,000 of tax losses from depreciation less $100,000 of taxable income on sale). But, your cash investment is now worthless — that's $100,000 out the window. If the net tax loss, $100,000, resulted in tax savings of $50,000, the real economic loss to you is $50,000.

So, if the investment is not worth what you paid for it, you lose.

The same tax concepts apply in a partnership, and the mechanics are fairly simple. If you include debt to determine the cost of the asset purchased, you have to include the debt in the proceeds from sale. So, the original cost of your discharged limited partnership interest includes your percentage share of partnership debts — even non-recourse debts. (Remember, these are obligations for which you have no personal liability.)

But, a reduction in partnership liabilities (relief from debt) is treated as a distribution of cash based on your percentage share of those liabilities. So, if you sell your partnership interest, the proceeds from the sale will equal your selling price plus your share of partnership liabilities. Subtract your tax basis as determined below, and the difference is the amount of your gain.

Here are the items that make up the tax basis in a partnership:

- A partner's tax basis includes all cash contributions plus his percentage share of partnership debt;
- Losses allocated to a partner and cash distributed to a partner reduce his basis;
- A reduction of debt is treated as a cash distribution;
- Losses in excess of basis aren't deductible and cash distributions in excess of basis are taxable;
- Profits increase a partner's basis.

When a partner's interest is sold, the gain equals the selling price plus the partner's share of partnership liabilities less the amount of adjusted tax basis.

There's a simple way to figure out how much you're on the hook for. Add up all tax losses and cash distributions from the first year you entered the partnership. Subtract all cash contributions (investment) you've made to the partnership. The difference, plus any cash you would receive upon sale, is the amount of your taxable gain (assuming the partnership never had taxable income).

Your tax liability will be equal to the taxes due on the gain. Some of the gain may be taxable as ordinary income (depreciation recapture) and some may be taxable as capital gain. Just remember that the IRS is vitally interested in learning by just how much those early tax losses exceeded your cash outlay. And, if they catch up to you, they will apply these rules to determine the amount of your tax liability.

It's contrary to human nature to consider that a business failure may create a taxable gain. More than one observer has suggested that a taxpayer either should experience a certain loss of memory when his tax shelter develops a leak or he should change accountants. Our advice is to concentrate primarily on economic value whenever considering a tax shelter investment in the first place.

INVESTIGATING TAX SHELTERS

DUE DILIGENCE IN TAX SHELTER INVESTMENTS

The objectives of "due diligence" are to develop confidence that the offering document contains full and fair disclosure and that the limited partner/investor has a shot at an economic profit. There are no guarantees, of course. But add these two elements to a properly conducted securities offering and your legal exposure drops if you are selling, advising on, or investing in tax shelters.

The term "due diligence" refers to the securities underwriter's, or participating dealer's, obligation to verify independently the facts and representations provided by a "seller" or "issuer" of securities. (As you read on, you'll see the process can be complicated and begin to understand why it's wise to buy tax shelters from investment dealers that go through the due diligence process for you.) Typically, the "seller" or "issuer" is the general partner in a limited partnership tax shelter. The ultimate securities law liability rests with the seller, so his legal counsel prepares the offering documents.

Much of the effort of the seller is spent creating an offering document that gets him off the hook. You're warned about every conceivable risk and trap. Most such documents give the general partner wide latitude and the investor no hope. It's definitely "caveat emptor." The document is called either a private placement memorandum, in the event the offering qualifies for exemption from registration under the securities law, or a prospectus ("red herring"), if the offering is registered for sale with the S.E.C.

The heavy weighting of disclaimers in offering memoranda frequently makes judging the economic merits of the transaction all but impossible for the unsophisticated.

Enter the first line of defense in tax shelter due diligence: It helps to know the basic business of the shelter so you can judge investment value and relative prices. If you know the business economics, the offering document usually contains enough relevant facts to give you a pretty good idea whether the proposition makes sense. So stick with investments in businesses you understand.

Second, you can request additional information not in the offering document that you deem necessary for a more complete understanding of the transaction. To give a few examples: You can ask for references and industry contacts; budgets and forecasts to get a picture of the general partner's financial health; key personnel compensation methods; investment philosophy and prior activities; and you can interview the general partner's counsel, accountants and past investors (phone calls will do).

Inquire about conflicts of interest, and see how the general partner intends to handle them. Here is an area in which you should not settle for the broad language in the offering memorandum.

It's a good idea to have the general partner, or the underwriter, provide a Dun and Bradstreet report on the people and companies involved. Also, check with the national and regional S.E.C. offices and the State Securities Commission. If a private placement is involved, you should expect the issuer's counsel to provide an opinion that the offering is exempt from registration.

A visit to the general partner's headquarters is helpful. Then you can directly evaluate the depth and the quality of the people involved. Are these the kind of people you want to be in business with? If you know enough about it, you can look into management information systems and accounting procedures. You should review reporting to limited partners in past deals and the system for handling investor inquiries.

Naturally, compare what you learned in these steps with what's in the prospectus. There should be no material omission or misstatements. If you discover inconsistencies, ask the sellers' counsel to explain them.

Finally, pay attention to the terms of the transaction which are usually complicated. Here, you should not worry about one of the terms in isolation but all the terms together. The fairness of terms in tax shelter deals varies widely, but focus on the overall transaction. The more deals you look at, the better judge of terms you'll be. Use common sense. For instance, in real estate, if you're paying a fully developed price for a property under construction, be sure the seller is locked into delivering the building performing as promised.

On a less esoteric level, here are Andrew Tobias' rules on tax shelters:

- Never go into a tax shelter deal in a panic at the last minute. This is the surest way to get burned.
- Never go into a deal that, were it not for its supposed tax benefits, would be unattractive.
- Never go into a deal that seems too good to be true.
- Avoid deals that seem particularly 'cute' or bizarre. (The more offbeat, the more likely to attract IRS attention.)
- Always ask yourself why, if the deal is so good (or good at all), they are offering it to you.
- Avoid deals that are based outside the United States.
- Be aware that, other than in real estate, there is no longer any purpose to a non-recourse loan. So if you do sign a note as part of the purchase price of participation in a shelter, you might someday have to make good on that note, no matter how badly the deal has gone.
- Beware of deals that seem to have no economic function besides avoiding taxes. If that's how it looks to you, that's probably how it will look to the IRS, too.

—Esquire, March 17, 1979

Oil & Gas

The three landmines in oil and gas deals recently have been outright fraud, improper cost allocations and co-mingling of funds or diverting them from the intended use. The trouble from a due diligence point of view is that all three are hard to uncover without a separate audit which is prohibitively expensive and time consuming. But, there are areas you can look into.

- Track Record - If the general partner has continuity of personnel and area of operations, the past record can be a guide to future performance. Ask about turnover of professional staff and where drilling dollars will be spent compared with previous years. Look at the record of future net revenues from proven reserves only, confirmed by an independent engineer, escalated modestly at an 8% or 10% rate but to a maximum price of about $60 per barrel ($10 per Mcf), and discounted to present value at 10%. Chop the result by 1/3 as a risk discount. The resulting figure, plus cash distributions to date, should at least equal limited partner capital contributions plus assessments plus debt. Use a weighted average over the past five years.

- Drilling Philosophy - Ask about the nature of proposed drilling in terms of risk and the pattern of expenditure. Wells may be categorized as developmental or exploratory, but there are many gradations of risk in between. Some are defined as exploratory for S.E.C. purposes but are much closer to a developmental level of risk. Remember, diversification is a key element. And as for expenditures, some programs plan to spend the entire limited partner capital contribution on initial exploration and finance resulting development work from assessments, borrowings and reinvested cash flow. Unless enormous reserves are discovered (a real long shot based on the program industry's past record), this approach doesn't pay off in present value terms for the investor.

- Prospect Selection - Ask what the prospect selection criteria are. The best screening approach is making what is known as a "risk adjusted return" calculation net to the limited partner. Here, the estimated success ratio and the probability of a given level of oil and gas reserves are multiplied by the projected recoverable hydrocarbon accumulation. Given a price assumption, resulting reserve values can then be calculated for the limited partner after the general partner's cut and the front-end load. These net risk-adjusted reserve values should be compared to the limited partner's investment in the prospect. The exercise should show a return in the three or four to one range if product prices for reserve values are escalated and in the two or two and one-half to one range on flat, or current, prices.

- Allocations - One way or another, the general partner will be reimbursed for most costs in running the program. But the variations are endless, and some methods are unreasonable. Space does not permit more than noting the items. The general partner's overhead is divided into categories such as leasehold costs, exploration, production and development, program administration and corporate overhead. The questions to ask: What is the system of overhead allocation, and how much is allocated to programs? Are amounts reasonable by industry standards? With respect to drilling costs and drilling and producing well supervision fees, how and when are payments made and are programs treated similarly to other working interest owners?

- General Partner - The program business is complicated, requires capital and involves certain inherent conflicts of interest. Be sure the general partner is managing his own business properly in terms of budgeting and forecasting. He needs capital for lease and prospect inventory, working capital, obligations to partnerships and satisfaction of the so-called "safe harbour" net worth test (if his corporation is the sole general partner of the program). Conflicts involve selling supplies and services to the program, drilling for the corporate account away from the programs, promoting leasehold inventory on behalf of the general partner and handling of funds.

Real Estate

"Original sin" in a real estate deal is overpaying badly for the asset. One object of due diligence in real estate is to determine the real value of the acquired asset. Usually the eyes are glazed over by the prospect of large tax losses per dollar of investment, especially in private placements. Except for subsidized housing and net leases, large tax losses are not available in real estate deals unless you overpay for the asset or take a very aggressive tax posture. Other problems to watch out for are inadequately financed partnerships, builders going broke, diversion of funds, and projections not materializing for properties under construction. By and large, publicly registered pooled funds have been relatively free of such problems.

- Acquisition Philosophy - A key consideration is acquisition personnel and their compensation. Real estate deals generally involve thorough screening and protracted negotiation. One man cannot acquire intelligently more than four or five properties a year. Acquisition files should include cost studies, pro forma operating statements, figures on comparable properties, independent appraisals and real estate documents. Usually, front-end loads are significant and can only be absorbed if properties are acquired well (cheaply). One problem with real estate tax shelters is the high level of acquisition fees relative to the residual values earned by the general partner. The fee structure emphasizes buying properties to the possible exclusion of subsequent performance. There are significant regional differences in prices, and different types of property have wide variations in risk, current return and appreciation potential. Acquaint yourself and be comfortable with the acquisition philosophy of your general partner.

- Management - You are not acquiring "bricks and mortar" but a small business enterprise. The property requires all kinds of decisions — when to replace the carpet, boiler or roof; what rent to charge; which tenants to accept; whether to make improvements; and when to refinance or sell. Each will be critical in determining or creating increased value. You should look at financial control procedures and information systems, budgets and variances, marketing plans and engineering and maintenance staff. In addition to property management, the nature and scope of the general partner's activities are obviously critical. Does he employ real estate people (mortgage bankers, property managers, loan administrators, appraisers, engineers, etc.) or primarily stockbrokers and lawyers? You need to know the sources of his income, banking and lending relationships, internal accounting and controls, and net worth for "safe harbour" purposes.

- Deal Terms - Unfortunately, even if the underlying acquisition effort is finely tuned and carefully executed, the game can be lost on the way to the limited partner's cash. Some techniques are suspicious, such as successive property transfers, carve-outs of land values and cash flow, interposing of second mortgages (or wraparounds) and excessive markups (40% is stiff, 15% to 25% is fair). Many times the investor is paying a fair price for a developed property but the builder (not the general partner) is only obligated to complete the building and meet minimal economic tests. The real risk is left with the limited partner as to whether the property ever justifies the purchase price. The syndicator contributes the acquisition contract, collects substantial fees and assumes no real obligation with respect to the property. Obviously, determining how the general partner has handled past problems and difficulties is a prime ingredient in judging his suitability for future syndications.

- Delivering Economic Results - The real test is whether or not the limited partner has received what's been promised. Have projections of tax consequences and property economics been met? What's the value of the limited partner's position In past deals? What were the financial results with liquidated properties or partnerships? Be careful to value realistically any mortgages taken back on sale.

TAX SHELTER TURN-OFF CHECKLIST

The client wants advice on buying a tax shelter, but as an accountant or a lawyer you may feel unqualified, or ethically and legally restrained, from giving an investment opinion. Sure, you can evaluate the tax consequences, but your business probably does not include providing investment advice or services. And, you're probably not licensed to do so. The tax shelter turn-off checklist detailed in the following pages can give you constructive guidance in screening out the problem shelters while helping you retain the client.

Or, you're an investor and you must make an investment decision. You can use the checklist too. This checklist is basically for private placements and it is designed to help you weed out the time wasters and the tempting but troublemaking investments. As background, you should know that audit risks are very high for returns with deductions from abusive shelters. (See: "IRS — The Bark and the Bite" on page 9.) You must have exceptional confidence in the shelter or be very sophisticated if you contemplate tax shelter investment in the current IRS targets: book and record masters; lithographic plates; movies; T.V. programs; cattle; minerals; and investment and commodity straddles.

Nine Points

Here is our tax shelter turn-off check list — nine key points to consider to help avoid pitfalls in tax shelter investing.

- Method of Solicitation - If you were introduced to a shelter by cold call, direct mail, coupon response, or boiler room techniques, look no further. Undoubtedly, for a private placement you have been illegally solicited. That's a bad start for a serious investment. The oil futures schemes of the past few years fraudulently raised millions through these selling techniques.

- The Non-Securities Offering - Here you're offered the direct purchase of solar panels, energy-saving devices, licenses, patents, art-masters, "gold for taxes" and gizmos of all sorts. There's no offering document because the seller claims he's not offering securities. The main reason the promoter seeks to avoid categorization as an issuer of securities is to escape securities law regulations and related sanctions and disclosure of his prior performance record and activities. According to the SEC, however, most of these deals require registration because they are (i) investments contracts and are (ii) sold like securities. In addition to the legal complications, these programs generally have no economic reality. If you get involved with this kind of deal, you face serious risks.

- Fees Not Commissions - Sure, an accountant or lawyer can look at a deal a client brings in and charge him a fee. But, promoters have been known to offer to pay the professional a "review" fee or reimburse the client for paying such a fee. This practice generally is the mark of a questionable shelter for two reasons. In a recent Revenue Ruling the IRS described such fees as commissions, and both the IRS in a Private Letter Ruling and the Tax Court have raised substantial questions about expensing even legitimate "professional fees" if the professional brings the investment to the client (as opposed to the client bringing the investment to the professional for review). Secondly, the NASD says non-NASD licensed "professionals" cannot accept such fees in connection with a transaction because these fees are commissions which only licensed people (including those with the special SECO broker license) can take. The NASD claims this area represents the biggest regulatory problem in tax shelters today.

- Absence of Known Experts - One essential protection for the investor is adequate and accurate disclosure of material facts in the offering memorandum. Such disclosure is most assured when well-known accountants, lawyers or financial intermediaries are involved in preparing the document. The possible exception is if you know the sponsor or the principals or if you are very knowledgeable about the business of the shelter.

- Multiple Losses, Limited Liability - Remember the "at-risk" rules. You have to be really liable for any debt to claim losses in excess of your actual cash investment (except for real estate.) So usually multiple write-off deals (except real estate) are economically absurd. Promoters may promise multiple losses and suggest that one way or the other your liability won't exceed your cash investment even if you guarantee debt. But, arrangements to insure against loss, cancel debt, extend payment way into the future, hold assets aside from claims, pay debt only from the business results of the shelter, etc., do not provide a basis for tax losses to be larger than cash investment.

- ITC Shelters (also characteristic of the "Non-Securities Offering" category) - If the promoter promises half, or more, of your money back from investment tax credits ("ITC"), you're probably buying the asset at an inflated price, and the tax credit won't stand up. The ITC is based only on "fair market value," not a high contrived value. Our favorite is the record master deal that assigned a value of $250,000 to the asset for the purposes of calculating the 10% tax credit while showing only $60,000 of gross revenues from royalties during the first seven years of ownership! A second factor to consider in ITC shelters is that there are limits on the amount of ITC you can take. The limit is equal to 10% of the at-risk amount. But the at-risk amount only includes borrowings if the lender is a third party.

- No Prior Performance Record - One of two disturbing possibilities can account for the absence of a "Prior Activities" section in a tax shelter offering document. One is obviously that the general partner hasn't had any past experience in the business! Hardly a comfort. The other is that the promoters are using the multi-corporate entity dodge. A newly formed corporation is the general partner of each partnership and therefore lacks a track record for purposes of the offering documents. Reputable counsel would undoubtedly insist on enumerating in the offering memorandum other corporate affiliates controlled by the same people and involved in similar businesses; but the unscrupulous often cut this corner.

- Fancy Economic Claims - Or, remembering Andrew Tobias' admonition, "If it's too good to be true, it is." Legitimate tax shelters are not promoted with wild claims and exaggerated projections. Use your common sense. Shallow gas development wells will not produce a riskless five for one return on investment. If they could, you'd never be offered one to drill.

- Suitability - The best approach to buying shelters is to plan an investment portfolio that puts money to work over several years in several shelters. So you should contact an investment professional and line up a diversified source of product. Above all, don't expect miracles. Remember some rules: One shot income (or income subject to big fluctuations) is hard to shelter; capital gains can't be sheltered efficiently; preference items can make deferral shelters inappropriate for some investors.

Additional Advice

We estimate that $8 billion of tax shelters (defined as limited partnership offerings or direct placement programs) were sold in 1981. These partnerships represent investment alternatives perceived to provide an inflation hedge with tax benefits a secondary consideration. About eighty percent were either oil and gas or real estate partnerships, with the balance primarily equipment leasing. Sixty to sixty-five percent of the total were registered with the SEC. For the publicly offered portion, the average tax loss in the year of investment probably did not exceed 40% of cash contributions (higher in oil and gas, lower in real estate) — hardly sufficient tax incentive to make ignoring investment values wise.

With tax shelter investments, you have basically two courses of action. You can develop a knowledge of asset and business values and be active enough in the area to understand relative business terms for these transactions. This way you can determine if the assets are being acquired at a fair price with customary formulas for sharing revenues and costs between limited and general partners. Or, you can arm yourself with the questions to ask the sponsor to get a proper evaluation of the investment.

COMMON MISTAKES IN TAX SHELTER INVESTING

Tax shelters are by and large long-term investments. The underlying business is usually at an early stage of development and doesn't achieve full value for years. The limited partnership interests are not readily resaleable. But, often the taxpayer's focus is short-term: How can I get Uncle Sam off my back this year?

Sole concentration on the immediate tax loss characteristics of a tax shelter is an all-too-common and, unfortunately, serious mistake. Indeed, through a variety of devices, tax losses can be anything you want them to be if you're willing to substantially overpay for the assets of the business. But tax losses are simply a form of borrowing from the U.S. Treasury — they are repaid eventually. Why pay too much for assets at the start for tax losses you don't keep when you wind up the investment?

Most investors are far better served by selecting shelters based on investment or economic merit. The ultimate value of the asset is the most important element in determining your real rate of return. The following discussion notes some of the common mistakes and misconceptions in tax shelter investing.

"Look, It's A Tax Shelter. I Need The Losses. That's Why I Bought It."

Reality: It's amazing how often everyone involved in "high write-off" tax shelters acknowledges from the start there's no business reality in the transaction. That's a foolish approach now. The IRS intends to audit one in every four partnership returns showing aggregate losses over $25,000, and that's practically any shelter you'll see. The IRS is less and less willing to settle through negotiation and more likely to force investors into court. So the odds of getting caught are much higher.

"The Bigger The Tax Loss The Better The Deal."

Reality: Big tax losses only show up when assets are overpriced or when big tax risks are present. (Real estate is still the only legitimate multiple write-off remaining.) The more you pay for an asset the higher the depreciation and/or investment tax credit. Tax shelters are the only game in town where it might seem the higher price you pay the better the deal. But tax credits and depreciation must be based on "fair market value" to stand up. The promises in the offering memorandum don't always make it through an audit. And, common sense should tell you paying more can't be as good as paying less.

"Some Deal! Ninety-Nine To One Leverage."

Reality: The property costs $10 million to build; the mortgage is $9.9 million. Ninety-nine to one leverage? Hardly. The limited partners put up $3 million. The correct view: the total cost is $13.0 million, so the mortgage is 76% of the total ($9.9 ÷ $13). One way you gain high leverage is for the general partner/promoter to take back a mortgage on the property or asset. Usually this arrangement (called a wrap-around mortgage) is the sure sign you're paying too much for the property. You're also probably giving the promoter the income and most of the potential appreciation of the property. That's too high a price to pay for tax shelter.

"I Got Around The At-Risk Rules."

Reality: If you think you did, so will the IRS. The "at-risk" rules limit losses to cash investment or its equivalent. You actually have to guarantee debt to be able to take tax losses larger than your cash investment — regardless of what the offering memorandum says. Any other arrangement, stated or implied, will knock out the loss. And, the business venture better be sound, or you'll have to repay the debt personally as well.

"They Told Me I Can Avoid Recapture By Giving The Shelter Away When The Tax Lines Cross."

Reality: The only foolproof way to avoid most recapture (defined as taxation of losses previously taken upon the sale or disposition of the shelter) is to die. That's quite a price to pay. Any other time you give away an asset with items subject to recapture, the transfer will probably be considered part sale and part gift, and you'll be taxed on the recapture portion. Even worse, assets encumbered by debt create special problems. The difference between your tax basis and the debt outstanding will be considered taxable gain if you give the asset away. Only the excess value of the shelter over the debt amount will constitute the gift portion.

"I Only Go For No-Risk Shelters."

Reality: The only no-risk shelter is a donation of cash to a charity. If the tax shelter business venture truly has little risk, the return will be less than a municipal bond.

"Going Through Stock Brokerage Firms Is Too Expensive. I Buy Shelters Locally."

Reality: All the ridiculous, outrageous and fraudulent tax shelters we see are "done locally." True, so is a good one occasionally. You may be savvy enough to investigate and decide about the merits of a deal yourself. But many times there are hidden mark-ups in local deals, and the terms can be much more onerous because of the lack of arms length negotiation. The best advice is stay with transactions from reputable financial intermediaries.

"Shelters Are Everywhere. Just Pick Up The Phone Or Answer An Ad."

Reality: You should recognize coupon ads, cold telephone calls and the salesman's "too-good-to-be-true" promises for what they are: boiler room sales techniques, fraudulent selling practices and violations of securities offering laws. If the promoters of a shelter will break those laws, imagine what else they'll do to you. If you don't know the general partner, the sponsor or the seller, don't buy the shelter!

"I'll Wait Until Later In The Year To Buy My Shelters. My Tax Picture Will Be Clearer."

Reality: Good thought, as far as it goes, but typically the proportion of questionable deals increases dramatically later in the year. For one thing, when you're desperate you may buy anything and are usually offered the opportunity. For another, tax laws favor tax shelter investment early in the year, and many of the good ones have come and gone by Memorial Day. Be careful after Labor Day, avoid the impulse after Thanksgiving and take a vacation after Christmas. For real estate shelters, the end of the year can be a good time to make an investment—but for next year's losses.

"I Only Need Shelter This Year."

Reality: If your income is truly unpredictable, no shelter may be appropriate for you. If your large income this year comes from capital gains, you have to be particularly careful about tax shelters. That's because of a tax called the Alternative Minimum Tax. To oversimplify, with large gains you can shelter the amount of your non-gain income efficiently — but not the taxable portion of the gain. You should see a competent tax advisor.

"Look At This Schedule Of Losses. I'll Hardly Have Any Cash In The Deal."

Reality: Subtle but aggressive tax approaches can radically affect the tax losses portrayed but don't change prospects for the business of the partnership one bit. The only lasting value is in the asset you buy. So the investment or economic merit of a tax shelter is the most important factor to consider.

"Have I Got A Hot One. I'm Going To Mine Gold In French Guiana."

Reality: Beware of the esoteric or offbeat deal. The odds are strong that by the time it gets to you, it's well known to the IRS or the SEC too. And an adverse revenue ruling is probably seconds away. We've never seen any "wild one" that had a particle of substance to it. You can easily end up being denied the tax losses and losing your capital too. Also, beware of a tax shelter that mixes different kinds of business activities. Usually each element won't stand up on its own, so you shouldn't expect them to make sense together.

"I Only Buy Deals With A 25% Or Higher Rate Of Return."

Reality: There are more ways to calculate rates of return than there are tax shelters. The method of calculation can easily double the return figure you're shown. Expected real returns should be somewhat higher for tax shelters than for other successful marketable long-term investments. That's your compensation for the illiquidity and the risk. But beware when extraordinary returns are advertised for tax shelters. They just don't exist, and you're probably being over-sold.

"It Must Be Good. They Raise A Lot Of Money." Or, "It Must Be Good, So And So Is In."

Reality: Unfortunately, in the tax shelter business, raising a lot of money usually means a highly skilled sales force and doesn't necessarily signify quality merchandise. In fact, some of the biggest frauds succeed in wide promotion. And one word, "Homestake", (a famous $100 million fraud that sucked in many an unsuspecting Chairman of the Board as an investor) should be enough to discredit the "who's who" theory. Further, you may find the well-known investor also owns part of the general partner/sponsor/promoter, just possibly indicating some loss of objectivity.

OIL AND GAS TAX SHELTERS

WHY YOU SHOULD DRILL FOR OIL AND GAS

Remember the earlier example of what's happened to oil and gas prices and well drilling costs over the last nine years. What those numbers reveal is a dramatic improvement in the economics of drilling. Oil and gas prices at the wellhead have risen more than four times as fast as drilling costs since the Arab oil embargo in 1973.

An index of drilling costs reveals a 187% increase in drilling contractor prices and a 134% increase in the price of purchased items since 1973. The weighted average cost increase is 154%, or an average of 22% per year through 1980.

About 40% of drilling costs are made up of payments to drilling contractors based upon the day or footage rate to rent the drilling rig and crew. About 60% of the cost to drill and complete a well is for purchased items such as site preparation, drilling mud, casing and tubing, tool rental, wellhead equipment, etc.

The price of oil in 1973 was $4.25 per barrel. The price today is about $32, an 800% increase. The price of natural gas in 1973 was about 48 cents per Mcf (thousand cubic feet). Today, newly discovered gas is about $2.90, a 600% increase. Free market gas from Mexico and Canada is $4.47 per Mcf, 830% higher than in 1973. And, gas produced from below 15,000 feet is now approximately $8.50 per Mcf.

With prices up 800% and costs up 154%, the result is a dramatic increase in potential return on investment. The successful search for oil and gas is much more profitable today than it has been in years.

The table below translates these price changes to drilling profit. Assume you discover a well with the same quantity of natural gas today as you found in 1973, say 3 million Mcf. The discovery is worth $6.9 million dollars today versus $900,000 then.

Economics of a Gas Well
(000's)

	1973	1981
Gas Discovered (Mcf)	3,000	3,000
Price (Dollars/Mcf)	x $.48	x $2.90
Recoverable Reserve Value	$1,440	$8,700
Drilling Costs	-420	-1,066
Operating Costs	-120	-780
Profit On The Well	$ 900	$6,854
Ratio of Profit to Drilling Cost	2.1/1	6.5/1

Price Outlook

The price of natural gas rises with inflation under the Natural Gas Policy Act of 1978. This act regulates prices of 31 different categories of natural gas until 1986 when a free market for most gas prices will take over. Until then, maximum allowable prices increase at the rate of inflation plus several percentage points for newly discovered gas — so-called "Section 102" gas.

For this category, The American Gas Association recently projected price increases per million BTU's (roughly equivalent to an Mcf) to $3.67 in 1985. This estimate is based upon an inflation rate of 7.4% per year during this period. And, higher inflation rates will translate to even higher allowable gas prices.

There's some talk of upward adjustment in allowable natural gas prices. Prices were set when domestic oil was $16 per barrel, not the current $32 figure. On a price per BTU basis, gas is one-half as expensive as oil. No wonder all our neighbors are converting to gas. The outlook for gas prices is very good. What about oil?

The world will have to accommodate a declining supply of oil within five years. That's quite a switch from an oil supply that grew 5½% per year for 50 years prior to 1973. The reasons according to British Petroleum (B.P.): First, the worldwide rate of new discoveries fails to match the decline in production from existing fields; and second, the U.S. response to the energy crisis is still uncertain.

The U.S. is the largest oil consumer and importer and the largest potential source of new energy supplies outside the Soviet Union. The adversary relationship between Congress and the industry makes suspect our ability to rise to the challenge of meeting the nation's energy needs. B.P. views the windfall profit tax as especially myopic in this regard.

A B.P. "White Paper" goes on to point out that 21% of the Free World's crude reserves are in four fields: two in Saudi Arabia, one in Kuwait and one in Venezuela. The newest one is 28 years old.

No super giant fields (reserves greater than five billion barrels) have been discovered in the 1970's. To maintain the present level of production, two Alaskas or one North Sea are required every year. The outlook seems clear. Increasing prices with declining reserves will be the order of the day for the long term.

Granted declines in domestic crude oil prices did appear in 1981. These declines are a natural short-term response to spot market factors. Storage tanks are full. Demand has declined due to the recession in the U.S. And, conservation has been effective. OPEC set a price of $34 per barrel through the end of 1982. But, the world can produce 6 or 7 million barrels of oil per day more than current demand. Dramatic increases in oil prices seem unlikely in the next several years barring major political disruptions.

The drilling funds are considered to be largely a natural gas play anyway. Perhaps 65% or more of discovered reserves have been natural gas. That's to your benefit since the price outlook for gas is superior to oil over both the short-term and through 1986.

The Impact of the Windfall Profit Tax

If you're a limited partner in a drilling investment, the windfall profit tax probably won't seriously impact today's favorable economics of drilling. For one thing, you are entitled to the lowest rate of tax if you're an "independent producer" (defined as producing less than 1000 barrels of oil daily). And, each limited partner, rather than the partnership, is defined as an independent producer. This is also true for purposes of the depletion allowance. Independents are allowed full percentage depletion on revenues subject to the tax, and this further reduces its impact.

Part of the selling price, called the base price, is exempt from the tax. The base price rises with inflation or even faster for some properties. Theoretically, the windfall profit tax will phase out after 1988 or 1991.

The windfall profit tax is actually an excise tax, not applied to profits. The tax is deductible from gross income and is applied only against the difference between the prices you receive for your oil and the applicable "base price" adjusted for state severance taxes and inflation. Starting base prices vary.

Remember: The windfall profit tax only applies to oil production, not natural gas. Natural gas prices are controlled by the Natural Gas Policy Act of 1978, but prices are allowed to increase with inflation or even faster in some cases.

NEW TAX ACT IMPROVES OIL AND GAS INVESTMENT RETURNS

The new tax rate reductions mean two things — tax deductions from oil and gas investments save less taxes, and oil and gas income is taxed at lower rates. The net impact of ERTA favors the investor.

Your at-risk investment increases $600 to $800 for each $10,000 of investment, but your after-tax income increases $1,950 up to $3,250 depending on your tax bracket (assuming a successful program). Net tax savings don't drop as much as the 23% effective drop in tax rates, because the cost of tax preference items should be largely eliminated in the new law.

In successful programs, the rates of return are about the same in lower tax brackets as in high tax brackets. And even a "1 to 1" deal, with net future revenues equal to investment, can return more than your investment after tax. The reason: Your rate of tax savings on the deduction is higher than the tax rate you will pay on oil and gas income (thanks to the depletion allowance).

Higher Returns

The good news — the reduction in tax rates dramatically improves the amount of oil and gas income you keep on an after-tax basis. The return goes up because the effective tax rate on income goes down. For the $215,000 taxable income individual (joint return), the effective rate on oil and gas income drops from 57% under the old law to 41% under the new law; for an individual with $60,000 of taxable income (joint return), the rate drops from 41% to 31%. The result is a substantial improvement in after-tax income.

The high income individual generates $3,250 more after-tax income in a "2 to 1" oil and gas program under the new law. The lower bracket individual increases his after-tax income

$1,950. That's a 37% improvement for the higher bracket investor and a 16% improvement for the lower bracket investor. Compare the after-tax cash flow under the old and new law.

Oil And Gas After-Tax Income
("2 to 1" Result on a $10,000 Investment)

CALCULATION OF TAXABLE INCOME

Future Gross Revenues	$25,000
Less: Operating Expenses	-5,000
Future Net Income	$20,000
Less: Depletion Allowance (1)	- 3,750
Taxable Income	$16,250

	$60,000 Income Bracket		$215,400 Income Bracket	
	Old Law	New Law	Old Law	New Law
Taxable Income	$16,250	$16,250	$16,250	$16,250
Tax Bracket	x 50%	x 38%	x 70%	x 50%
Tax Due	$ 8,125	$ 6,175	$11,375	$ 8,125
Future Net Income	$20,000	$20,000	$20,000	$20,000
Less: Tax Due	-8,125	-6,175	-11,375	-8,125
After-Tax Cash Flow	$11,875	$13,825	$ 8,625	$11,875
Effective Tax Rate (2)	41%	31%	57%	41%
Increased Cash Flow Under the New Law		$1,950		$3,250

(1) 15% of gross revenues - the percentage depletion rate for 1984 and thereafter.
(2) Tax due divided by future net income.

More At Risk

The after-tax cost of an oil and gas investment increases, but the big tax rate drop has less effect than you would think. As the table below shows, with $60,000 of taxable income, your at-risk investment increases by only $595 after tax for a $10,000 investment under the new law. Similarly, the increase is $850 for the $215,000 taxpayer. Notice the amount at risk goes up much less than the improvement in after-tax income.

Oil And Gas Investment Amount At Risk
(Per $10,000 Of Original Investment)

	\$60,000 Of Income			\$215,400 Of Income		
	Old Law	New Law	Change	Old Law	New Law	Change
Tax Loss	$ 8,500	$ 8,500		$ 8,500	$ 8,500	
Tax Rate	x 50%	x 38%		x 70%	x 50%	
	$ 4,250	$ 3,230	$ -1,020	$ 5,950	$ 4,250	$ -1,700
Preference Tax on I.D.C.	-425	0	425	-850	0	850
Net Tax Savings	$ 3,825	$ 3,230	$ -595	$ 5,100	$ 4,250	$ -850
Amount At Risk*	$ 6,175	$ 6,770	$ +595	$ 4,900	$ 5,750	$ +850

*Original investment less net tax savings.

Footnote: Intangible Drilling Costs (I.D.C.) for successful wells are tax preference items. We assumed a 50% success rate on wells drilled to calculate the additional tax. Under the old law, the preference items caused up to a 20% shift in tax rate for the taxpayer who had high earned income. This shifting effect of tax preference items for earned income taxpayers has been eliminated under the new law.

HOW TO SELECT A GOOD OIL AND GAS PROGRAM

There are a bewildering number of oil and gas drilling programs, and on the surface they all look pretty much the same. The good news is that nothing is further from the truth. The bad news is that even the good ones can have a bad year.

Over the years, we've developed a set of guidelines designed to produce superior investment results. These guidelines are broadly applicable and may be used to analyze any potential oil and gas investment. However, some of the needed information is unavailable to you in writing within current securities regulations. That's why it's always best to make this kind of an investment through a reputable financial intermediary such as a well-known brokerage firm. You may have to rely to some extent on verbal information, so deal with people you can trust.

The Past Record

The most important information is the drilling company's past record of performance. You should measure the record only one way—compare the future net revenues from proved oil and gas reserves in past programs in relation to limited partner capital contributions. Future net revenues are sales of oil and gas less the estimated operating and projected capital costs. The limited partner's capital contribution is original investment plus any assessments.

Frequently, results for oil and gas limited partnerships are expressed as a "3 to 1 Program," "2 to 1 Program," etc. This is the limited partner's expected future net oil and gas revenues (less any partnership debt) compared to his capital contribution. Beware: The revenues used in this calculation can be computed in a variety of ways. Normally, undiscounted proved reserves with product prices escalated for inflation are used for comparison purposes.

Essentially, a good track record should show an average of at least "2 to 1" for all the company's programs over the past three to five years. However, an even better indication of solid performance, if you can obtain the figures, is about 1.4 times investment in future net revenues from proved reserves discounted at a rate of 10%.

This important information is not found in most oil and gas prospectuses. Among the major drilling programs, only about ten include it. You can and should obtain at least a verbal representation of these figures from companies in which you intend to invest. You can adequately determine the economic success of prior programs only from this information.

Also, be sure you're comparing apples to apples. Only use proved reserves, not what are called probable or possible reserves. Examine the price escalation formulas and only use figures provided by an independent reserve engineering firm.

Success Ratios and Cash Tables

The past performance information provided in a prospectus, such as success ratios and cash distribution tables, is often either meaningless or hard to interpret.

The success ratio is the percent of all wells drilled that are completed as producing wells. A higher success ratio does not necessarily mean better economic results. Drilling in the Appalachian Basin (Ohio, West Virginia) should be successful 90% of the time versus a success ratio of 30% or 40% for drilling in Louisiana. Why drill in Louisiana? Reserves are more prolific and the return on investment potentially greater.

In one widely used program structure called "reversionary interest," the investor pays the completion costs as well as the intangible drilling costs. A low quality drilling company might complete a number of marginally economic wells with investor dollars. The success ratio table would therefore look good, but you could have a poor return on investment.

The cash distribution tables show the cash actually paid out to the investor. How can that possibly be deceiving? It's simple. Some types of wells pay (or produce) over 50% of all they'll ever pay out in the first two years of their productive life and don't produce any significant revenues after the first four years. Other types of wells produce a lower percentage in their early life but continue to produce over a twelve or fifteen year period at steady rates.

In order to properly evaluate the cash distribution information, you must know the specific characteristics of the producing sands which created the results shown for each of the prior programs. That's a more difficult and involved task than simply reviewing the economic results as represented by the future net revenue figures.

In addition to past record data, you need some sense that the company and technical personnel have experience in the program's area of operations. Here again you may have to ask because the prospectus probably won't tell you. But if you do ask, you'll get the answer. This is of critical importance because it's the continuity of experience that enables the past record to be translated into present and future performance.

The oil and gas business is very local in nature and the classic learning curve is a definite factor in performance. The more experience a drilling company has in an area, the better it performs. There are plenty of examples of fairly major drilling companies who drill in a new geological and geographic area only to face economic disaster in the early years. Two or three years later satisfactory results may appear. In the meantime, let them learn on someone else's dollar.

Who's Paying the Bills

Look for a deal where the drilling company is paying part of the bills. This will happen in one of two ways. First, the company could share all expenses across the board, a so-called "promoted interest" structure. Second, the company could pay the tangible costs leaving you to pay only the intangible drilling costs. This later cost sharing method is called a "functional allocation." Here are some reasons why these arrangements are good:

- They provide proof of financial capability. If the drilling company lacks the capital to pay its share of the bills, it may also lack adequate lease inventory, good staff, etc.;

- They result in more wells being drilled because the partnership has more capital. Observers of the drilling fund industry know a particular partnership's success almost always stems from two or three good discoveries (out of thirty to fifty wells drilled). Those extra wells count.

- In addition, the functional allocation arrangement creates higher tax losses, reducing the limited partner's "risk", since the drilling company pays all nondeductible costs. If you only pay intangible drilling costs, you can receive an 85% to 90% write-off in the year of your original investment versus a probable 60% write-off if you're paying both intangible and tangible costs.

Another factor to evaluate is how much of your capital contribution "goes into the ground" (a good rule of thumb should be at least 87.5%). This phrase applies to oil and gas drilling or leasing costs. Management fees, general and administrative overhead, brokerage commissions and offering costs don't go "into the ground" and are not actual drilling costs. If you're asked to pay more than 12.5% of your cash investment in front-end costs, you will dilute your chance of a good return on investment.

Diversify

When you read a headline that says "Texaco Drills $14.5 Million Dry Hole in Baltimore Canyon," you may think Texaco took a huge gamble. Read the last paragraph of the article. Texaco is what's known as the "operator" for a group of companies who jointly financed the well. Texaco's interest was probably 30% or less. In fact, as the risk and expense per well increase, Texaco — or any oil company — generally will own less of it. You should too — by diversifying.

Two measures of diversification are the number of wells in which the partnership invests and the total amount of the partnership's drilling budget. In this day and age, $10 million is a budget minimum. And, it's advisable to drill 30 wells or more. You can drill with several companies at the same time — but we prefer to drill with the same company over a period of several years. That way your result should more closely resemble the company's past record.

As a result of inflation, a $15 million drilling budget in 1981 only bought about as many "feet of hole" as $10 million bought in 1979. So an increased budget is certainly justified in part. But, often doubling or tripling available drilling dollars has doomed a good company to a mediocre result in the year of expansion.

So, beware of a rapidly expanding drilling budget. Money is easy to spend in the oil business but not so easy to spend wisely. Unfortunately, the critical variables that generally can't be increased rapidly are oil finding personnel and good prospects. Experienced oil finding people with a proven track record are in great demand. The same is true for lease prospects with a high probability for successful drilling results.

Guidelines

Here are some specific guidelines to help you evaluate a drilling fund company and improve your chances of success:

- Risks should be spread and hence reduced by diversifying geographically and geologically. In other words, wells should be located in different areas and drilled to various depths. The company should have an interest in over 25 wells.

- The company should show a success ratio of between 25% and 60% and be involved in semi-proven and "controlled" wildcat drilling. Wildcat drilling, as its name implies, is pure exploratory drilling with a maximum 30% chance of success. With semi-proven drilling, there's a 30% to 60% chance of success. Success is likely over 60% of the time for development wells but you generally pay more for these wells which reduces the economic returns.

- Funds should be raised in the first half of the year so that the program sponsor has ample time to line up drilling rigs and lease the prospects it needs. Moreover, raising funds in the first half allows at least partial development of any discoveries with cash already raised. By contrast, programs that raise funds in the second half of the year may experience rig-scheduling difficulties which can increase costs and threaten deductions. Prospect quality can also suffer, and borrowings may be required to provide the funds necessary for development of discoveries.

- In most programs, the general partner has the right to assess the limited partners for more funds. These assessments should be restricted to 25% or so and should only be used for development, not more exploration. There should also be limitations on raising additional funds by borrowing and on using cash generated by product sales for more drilling.
- A significant percentage of the program's prospects should be developed by in-house staff. This will tend to increase the program's net interest in a prospect.
- Cash distributions to the limited partner should start within 18 to 24 months after the program begins.
- At least 87.5% of the money put up by the limited partners should be spent on leases, geophysical work and drilling. The balance should be used to cover offering costs and pay overhead. The more of the investor's money actually spent on drilling activities, the better the program results should be. In some well-structured programs, as much as 93% or more of an investor's money is actually put to work in finding oil.
- Costs and tax deductions should be allocated along functional lines. The limited partners should pay the intangible drilling costs and other immediately deductible items. The general partner should pay the tangible drilling costs and other depreciable or amortizable costs. When a program results in completion of 40% or more of its wells, the general partner may contribute as much as 30% of the capital for a 40% share of revenues under this type of arrangement. The following chapter will explain functional allocation in greater detail.
- The revenue sharing arrangement should give the general partner incentive or "promotion" but a limitation of about a 15% promotion is best. The maximum promotion allowed the general partner by state securities law is a kicker of up to 25% more than the amount that would be received based upon the percentage of his capital contribution. Under this kind of arrangement, the general partner might receive a 40% share of the

revenues, even though he contributed only 15% of the capital. The limited partners would receive 60% of the revenues for contributing 85% of the capital. That's a bit expensive these days.
- Tax-deductible write-offs in the first year should amount to 85% of the money invested. Write-offs in the second year should be about 10% of the amount invested.

DEAL STRUCTURE DOESN'T COUNT

Arguments about deal structure in oil and gas programs are pure nonsense. The four commonly used deal structures for oil and gas programs produce about the same economic result to the limited partner. That's if the oil and gas finding record of the partnership is held constant. The difference is no more than plus or minus 10%. We've reached this conclusion by isolating deal terms as the only variable in comparing drilling programs. Specifically:

- The appropriateness of one deal structure versus another in an oil and gas program relates mainly to the type of drilling the partnership engages in;

- In a "Development" drilling program, the "Functional Allocation" arrangement provides noticeably better economics to the limited partner;

- In an "Exploratory" drilling program either a "Reversionary," "Carried" or "Promoted Interest" arrangement provides a much better economic result to the limited partner than a "Functional Allocation" arrangement;

- In a "Balanced" drilling program, the particular structure of the general partner's compensation doesn't affect the limited partner's economic result much at all;

- But, minor changes in the oil finding record are far more important than whatever deal structure you pick regardless of the type of drilling you do;

- Obviously, "Functional Allocation" cost sharing improves early year tax deductions regardless of the type of drilling because the limited partner only pays immediately deductible costs (intangible drilling costs).

Naturally, not all oil and gas programs are identically fair to limited partners. You should look for the best terms within the type of deal structure you favor and not be concerned whether that structure is better than another. Of course, the real answer is that the oil and gas finding record is the most important factor. Look there, and you'll improve your investment results.

Types of Deals Available

Four "standard" types of cost and revenue sharing arrangements are common in oil and gas drilling programs today. In the "Carried Interest" type the general partner will earn a substantial percentage of revenues (the average is 12.5%) from first commencement of production while paying only 1% of costs. Usually, after "payout" (return of limited partner investment in cash), the general partner's interest in revenues increases (the average is 16%).

In the "Functional Allocation" arrangement, intangible costs are paid by the limited partners and tangible costs are paid by the general partner. Here, revenues are typically split 60% to the limited partner and 40% to the general partner. In a "Promoted Interest" arrangement the general partner pays an average of 10% of all drilling costs across the board for 25% of revenues. The limited partner pays 90% of all costs for 75% of revenues. In the "Reversionary Interest" type the general partner has a 1% interest in costs and revenues before limited partner payout but a 25% interest after payout on average. The table on the next page shows the average business terms in oil and gas deals available today for these four structures.

Average Deal Terms

	Percent in Ground	Total Load	Cost Percentage Before Payout (1)	Cost Percentage After Payout (1)	Revenue Percentage Before Payout (1)	Revenue Percentage After Payout (1)
Carried Interest	84%	16%	99/1	99/1	87.5/12.5	84/16
Functional Allocation	90%	13%(2)	Intangible/tangible (4)		60/40	60/40
Promoted Interest	85%	17%(3)	90/10	90/10	75/25	75/25
Reversionary Interest	86%	14%	99/1	75/25	99/1	75/25

Footnote: The Average Deal Terms are a simple mathematical average of currently registered oil and gas programs judged to be in the four deal structure categories. Percent in ground - The percentage of limited partner investment used to pay actual drilling costs. Total load - The amount of front-end costs (sales commissions, management fees, etc.) paid by the limited partners.

(1) Limited partner percentage followed by general partner percentage.
(2) 3% paid out of revenues.
(3) 2% paid out of revenues.
(4) The general partner puts up all tangible (capitalized) drilling costs (generally no less than 15% of total costs) and the limited partner pays all intangible (deductible) costs.

First, we made some assumptions about development, balanced or exploratory oil and gas programs. We assumed no offset wells would be drilled in the development deal, one offset for two initially completed wells in the balanced deal and three offsets for each initially completed well in the exploratory deal. Other assumptions are outlined in the table below.

Assumptions For Type Of Drilling

	Development	Balanced	Exploratory
Lease Cost (1)	30%	20%	15%
Success Ratio:			
Initial Wells	80%	40%	20%
Subsequent Wells	None	75%	60%
Intangible Cost	$ 5,800	$10,060	$14,690
Tangible Cost	$ 4,200	$ 2,660	$ 2,310
Total Oil & Gas Expenditures (2)	$10,000	$12,720	$17,000
Future Net Revenues (3)	$25,000	$35,000	$40,000

(1) As a percentage of total oil and gas expenditure.
(2) Completed well cost is 70% intangible cost and 30% tangible cost, excluding lease cost.
(3) Three, five and six times completed well cost respectively.

Next, we superimposed the average business terms of the four deal structures on the assumptions for the three drilling objectives. Assuming identical investment in each, we calculated the ratios of future net revenues to limited partner investment. In other words, the oil and gas costs and results were identical within each type of drilling. The only variables were the deal terms. As you can see in the table on the following page, functional allocation was the clear winner in development and the loser in exploratory. The other three deal structures produced almost identical results no matter what the type of drilling.

**Ratio of Future Net Revenue
To Limited Partner Investment**

	Reversionary Interest (1)	Carried Interest (1)	Promoted Interest	Functional Allocation
Development	1.9/1	1.8/1	1.8/1	2.3/1
Balanced	2.0/1	2.0/1	2.2/1	2.0/1
Exploratory	2.0/1	1.9/1	2.0/1	1.7/1

(1) We assumed 12.5% lower revenues to the partnership to adjust for the probable lower net revenue interest generally available when sponsors use this deal structure.

The surprising result is the lack of difference for the limited partner in the twelve combinations.

Finally, the obvious conclusion — the ability to find oil and gas is much more important than the sponsor's deal structure. A 10% change in the success of drilling creates a greater variation in the investor's return than any change of deal structures. For instance, a 10% drop in future net revenues takes the promoted interest structure from the top ranking to the bottom in a balanced drilling program comparison.

Remember, the calculations above assume an "average" deal structure. A worse than average structure will affect negatively any investment you make.

RETURNS TO EXPECT FROM AN OIL & GAS INVESTMENT

A good oil and gas investment should provide a two to one ratio of future net revenues to investment. In other words, you hope your $10,000 investment creates a stream of cash distributions in future years of $20,000 or more. This is the so-called "two to one" program result. Income is partially taxable and partially tax free. That's because a portion of the income is considered a return of capital (the depletion allowance).

Economic benefits do not flow evenly over the life of an oil and gas program. The table on the following page adjusts the economic benefits (tax savings plus cash distributions) for time value by assuming reinvestment, at 6% after tax, of all economic benefits received until the end of the twelve-year life of a typical program.

After-tax returns always exceed the level of future net revenues. That's because tax savings are added in and because part of the return is represented by earnings on reinvestment of economic benefits. For instance, a 2.0 to 1 program for a taxpayer in the 60% bracket will produce an after-tax return of $25,468 on a $10,000 investment.

To illustrate how all of this works out, we have created an example based upon the following assumptions: The program will not borrow money or make any assessments; cash flow will begin in the third tax year following the initial investment — say, 1983 for a program that starts in 1981; approximately 90% of the future net revenues will be produced in the first 12 years of the program's life; operating costs will amount to 18% of gross income; the depletion allowance will fall to 15% by 1984 from a current level of 18%; and finally, tax savings plus cash distributions will be reinvested at a 6% annual compound rate after taxes. (It doesn't really matter what rate you use as long as you use the same rate to compare all investments.)

Returns On Oil And Gas Programs

Tax Bracket	After-Tax Returns Per $10,000			
	1.5/1*	2.0/1*	2.5/1*	3.3/1*
38%	$20,733	$25,900	$30,547	$38,286
50	21,241	25,421	29,625	36,265
60**	21,751	25,468	29,208	35,092

* Ratio of future net revenues to original investment.
**Possible through the addition of Federal, State and Local Taxes.

And, as you can see in the table, there is no substantial difference in the returns experienced by investors in the 38%, 50%, or 60% brackets. As future net revenues rise, so do returns for investors in lower tax brackets because more of the total return is represented by taxable dollars.

Hence, an investor in the 38% tax bracket is at least as "suitable" for an oil and gas investment as someone in the 60% tax bracket. This contradicts the conventional theory that higher tax bracket investors have a lower after-tax exposure to risk and hence are more suitable as investors in oil and gas programs.

Since a major portion of the income generated by an oil and gas program is taxable, it pays to find ways of easing the tax bite. Fortunately, there are some readily available means to allow an investor to improve his after-tax returns. For example, when the program's major tax benefits run out and it starts generating taxable income, you might consider gifting your interest to your children who are in a lower tax bracket than your own.

Or you might time your investment to maximize your after-tax return. For example, you might make periodic oil and gas investments during your last five working years. These are usually the peak earning years — and hence the peak tax bracket years. By the time you retire and are in a lower bracket, the energy shelters should start generating a cash return.

Stock portfolio performance has to be exceptional to match the return of an oil and gas drilling fund. You need at least a 14.3% pre-tax return per annum in equities to match the economic results of a 2.0 to 1 drilling program, assuming you're in the 50% tax bracket (adjusted gross income over $60,000 on a joint return).

The table below shows how well you would have to fare in a stock investment to match the after-tax results of the oil and gas investment shown in the table on page 74.

Compound Total Pre-Tax Return Required For Common Stock Investment To Equal Oil And Gas Investment

Tax Bracket	1.5/1*	2.0/1*	2.5/1*	3.3/1*
50%	11.9%	14.3%	16.3%	18.7%
60	12.1	15.3	16.9	19.1

* Ratio of future net revenues to investment.

Note: Common Stock return figures were calculated by compounding an estimated 6% dividend income after-tax at a 6% rate. Then, the compound rate of appreciation was determined so the sum of this appreciation adjusted for taxes plus the cumulative dividends after tax equaled the after-tax returns of oil and gas programs. The sum of the pre-tax appreciation rate plus the pre-tax dividend rate is the percentage shown in the table.

REAL ESTATE TAX SHELTERS

REAL ESTATE'S UNIQUE CHARACTERISTIC

What if you could find a business where 60% of your day-to-day expenses were fixed permanently for twenty-five or thirty years? Would you buy it? You bet you would. You're probably thinking there's no such thing. But, there is.

Leveraged real estate. It's that simple. Roughly 60% of on-going expenses in a leveraged real estate project are represented by interest and principal on the mortgage. These costs remain the same over 25 to 30 years — it's called the mortgage "constant." In an economic climate of continuing inflation, any business with a major portion of its expenses fixed will be a good investment.

There have been studies that suggest that commercial rents, specifically apartment rents, haven't kept pace with inflation which should mean cash flow squeezes for these properties. However, since only 40% of the annual costs of a real estate project are variable costs, such as operating expenses and taxes, rents need not rise as fast as the rate of inflation to preserve cash flow. So long as rents increase at 40% of the rate of inflation, cost increases will be covered.

Rents have been going up about 6% per year since 1970. This level of rent increase generates enough extra cash to cover a 15% increase in variable costs. Variable costs have been rising only 10% a year. So, cash flow from real estate projects should be increasing.

Assume a limited partnership purchases a 200 unit apartment complex for $34,000 per unit, or a total cost of $6,800,000. Also, assume you're able to obtain a permanent mortgage loan with a constant annual payment of interest and principal of 11.5%. The principal amount is $5,100,000— 75% of the cost of the property.

The limited partnership pays $1,700,000 in cash over the mortgage amount for the property, anticipating a cash on cash return of 6%, or $102,000 of cash distributions per year.

Let's take a look at a typical income statement:

Gross Potential Rent		$1,074,000
Vacancy Allowance (5%)		54,000
Rental Income		$1,020,000
Less: Operating Expenses		-180,000
Real Estate Taxes		-100,000
Management Fees		-51,000
Variable Costs		-$331,000
Operating Profit		$689,000
Less: Debt Constant		-587,000
Net Cash Flow		$102,000

The total costs include variable costs plus the debt constant. Operating expenses (cleaning, repairs and maintenance, utilities, snow and trash removal, payroll, real estate taxes and management fees) are all variable and will rise with inflation. The debt constant, which includes both the payment of interest and principal, doesn't change over the life of the mortgage. In this example, costs are 64% fixed and only 36% variable.

Operating Expenses	$180,000
Real Estate Taxes	+ 100,000
Management Fees	+ 51,000
Variable Costs	$331,000 (36%)
Debt Constant - Fixed Costs	+587,000 (64%)
Total Costs	$918,000 (100%)

This low proportion of variable costs for apartment projects is possible only if the tenants pay their own utility costs.

If the landlord pays all utilities (usually in older buildings), the variable costs would be significantly higher and represent a larger percentage of total costs. Apartment projects generally are the most expensive income property to operate.

In most commercial properties, total variable costs can be quite a bit lower. For instance, tenants in shopping centers typically pay their pro rata share of most operating expenses. And with office space, cost increases are often automatically passed through to tenants under so-called escalation clauses.

So the unique characteristic of leveraged real estate is the high percentage of fixed costs relative to total costs. But, this leverage can work both ways because total costs typically equal approximately 90% of rental income which leaves a pretty thin margin of profit.

For instance, in the previous example net cash flow was $102,000, or 10% of rental income ($1,020,000) after a 5% vacancy allowance. In other words, at 95% occupancy the project pays all its expenses and generates excess cash of $102,000 which is available for distribution to limited partners.

A quick way to determine the maximum break-even vacancy allowance (the point at which income generated is only sufficient to pay costs with no excess cash remaining) is to add the vacancy allowance to the cash flow and divide by gross rental income:

$$\frac{\$54{,}000 + \$102{,}000}{\$1{,}074{,}000} = 14.5\%$$

In this example 14.5% vacancy, or conversely 85.5% occupancy, represents breakeven operations. So a 10% drop in rental income from the projected 95% occupancy rate eliminates 100% of the cash return on your investment. That's operating and financial leverage working against you.

The Upside

As mentioned earlier, gross rents for broad categories of income-producing real estate have risen about 6% per year since 1970. But building operating costs have risen 10% a year — faster than the Consumer Price Index. That's principally because of the large amount of utility costs in building operating expenses.

Remember, only 40% of costs are variable. So, a 6% increase in gross rents per annum will offset a 15% increase in variable costs. And, a 6% increase in rents with a 10% increase in variable costs will result in an increase in cash flow.

Rental Income	$1,020,000	+ 6% =	$1,081,200
Operating Expenses	-331,000	+ 10% =	-364,100
Operating Profit	$689,000	+ 4% =	$717,100
Debt Constant	-587,000		-587,000
Net Cash Flow	$102,000	+ 27% =	$130,100

Notice that operating leverage is now working for you. An increase in operating profit of 4% improves your net cash flow by 27%.

It is unrealistic to expect this sort of rapid cash flow increase in real estate on a longer term basis. But, there is little doubt these factors are currently at work. So, a leveraged business with 60% or more of its costs fixed in a period of inflation is a very good investment.

THE BENEFITS OF
REAL ESTATE OWNERSHIP

You can obtain four different economic benefits by owning real estate — tax losses, cash flow, equity build-up and appreciation. Each occurs simultaneously and each adds to your net worth. The easiest to understand and most apparent is appreciation.

Real estate has been one of the prime beneficiaries of price inflation. Indeed, some argue, the demand for real estate is due in part to a worldwide flight from paper money into hard assets. This underlying trend affects the price of gold, paintings and diamonds as well as assets that produce current earnings such as real estate, oil and gas reserves and rail cars.

Real estate in the U.S. is still relatively cheap by world standards, and prices that seem high to us are quite reasonable to foreigners. Or, to put it another way, real estate inflation may have run its course abroad, but not in the U.S. The relative value of currencies affects the relative attractiveness of American real estate prices to foreigners.

Tax legislation has played an unintentional role in boosting real estate prices as well. No other asset or business gives an investor the ability to write-off more than his cash investment without being personally obligated for the additional amount. That's one result of the so-called "at-risk" provisions of the 1976 Tax Reform Act and the 1978 Revenue Act. Real estate has been singled out for favorable tax treatment and that has obviously increased demand.

Also, inflation makes the use of debt such as mortages very attractive for the borrower. However, new mortgage debt is hard to come by. Mortgage debt used to be available for up to three-quarters of the purchase price, and usually the loan was repayable over twenty-five years or more. Now, fixed rate loans are only available where the lender also owns a part of the equity in the property. Otherwise, mortgage loans carry variable interest rates and are due in eight or ten years.

Naturally, you hope the project you invest in will be able to increase rents faster than expenses increase. That will produce a higher level of earnings from the property and, if the earnings rise, so should the price at which you can sell the property. That is one way in which inflation increases property value. Another way is if a buyer's expectations of higher inflation lead him to pay a higher multiple for property earnings. Both factors have been at work in the real estate market lately.

The remaining three economic benefits of real estate are tax losses, cash flow and equity build-up. Let's look at the financial projections for an apartment property under construction to see clearly where these three other economic benefits come from.

The assumptions are as follows: The property will take eighteen months to build and eighteen months more to rent up; the principal amount of the permanent mortgage is $2,550,000 payable over 25 years; the mortgage constant is 11% annually (unrealistically low today but the example is used just to show sources of economic return); the equity investment (limited partner cash contribution) is $880,000; depreciation is calculated in accordance with the 200% declining balance method (only available for "subsidized" housing under ERTA of 1981); operating expenses are 30% of net rental income (tenants pay their own utilities); deductible fees equal $200,000 and other construction period expenses equal $480,000.

Income and expenses keep rising up to the probable date the property achieves projected occupancy. From that point on, the estimate of rents and expenses remains at a constant level until the property is sold (which is the same as estimating that future cost increases will be offset exactly by future rent increases).

This "stabilized" projection is the best method for evaluating new properties untested in the market. It is the approach the mortgage lenders will use to determine value for loan purposes. Reaching the point of stabilization may take three or four years from the date of original investment.

The Income Statement

The following table shows an abbreviated income statement. Revenues come from tenant rental income. There are five different categories of expenses:
- Operating expenses - including maintenance, property management, insurance, garbage removal, real estate taxes, common area utilities, etc.;
- Mortgage interest - that portion of debt service payments represented by deductible interest costs;
- Construction period expenses - expenses incurred before the building is occupied, such as real estate taxes, interest on the construction loan, etc. Some of these costs are not deductible when incurred and must be amortized over a period of years;
- Fees - frequently the seller of the property agrees to take a portion of his cash as payment for services, resulting in an immediate deduction for the buyer — for instance, guarantees for rent up, completion, financing, etc.;
- Depreciation - an accounting adjustment that compensates owners for the theoretical wear and tear and economic obsolescence of the property. Because of depreciation, a portion of the income you receive is considered a return of your capital investment and not subject to tax.

Apartment Project Income Statement (000's)

	1982	1983	1984	1985	1986	1987	1988	1989	1990	1991
Rental Income*	—	$100	$350	$500	$500	$500	$500	$500	500	500
Less:										
Operating Expenses	—	35	140	150	150	150	150	150	150	150
Mortgage Interest	—	131	260	258	256	254	251	248	245	241
Construction Period Expenses	$20	80	80	80	80	80	60	—	—	—
Fees	125	50	25	—	—	—	—	—	—	—
Depreciation**	—	99	190	175	161	148	136	125	115	106
Taxable Income (Loss)	($145)	($295)	($345)	($163)	($147)	($132)	($97)	($23)	($10)	$3

* After a 5% vacancy factor.
**Old ADR system — not new Accelerated Cost Recovery System.

The bottom line is taxable income or loss. That's the amount shown on your income tax return. If the bottom line is a loss, deduct the amount from your other income. Your taxes are reduced, and these tax savings represent one economic benefit of ownership.

The Cash Flow Statement

Only operating expenses and mortgage interest are paid in cash from property operations. The other three types of expenses are not. As a result, the income statement does not reflect the cash flow from property operations. The next table shows how to adjust the income statement to determine cash flow. Start with the taxable income or loss from the income statement. Then add:

- Construction period expenses and fees - these costs are normally paid when incurred from the limited partner capital contribution or from the mortgage proceeds but not from property operations;
- Depreciation - not a cash expense.

Also, mortgage principal payments represent a significant cash cost which is not deductible for tax purposes but must be subtracted before arriving at cash flow.

Apartment Project Cash Flow Statement (000's)

	1982	1983	1984	1985	1986	1987	1988	1989	1990	1991
Taxable Income (Loss)	($145)	($295)	($345)	($163)	($147)	($132)	($ 97)	($ 23)	($10)	$3
Add:[1]										
Construction Period Expenses	20	80	80	80	80	80	60	—	—	—
Fees	125	50	25	—	—	—	—	—	—	—
Depreciation*	—	99	190	175	161	148	136	125	115	106
Subtract:[2]										
Mortgage Principal Payments	—	(9)	(20)	(22)	(24)	(26)	(29)	(32)	(35)	(39)
Cash Flow (Loss)	—	($75)	($70)	$70	$70	$70	$70	$70	$70	$70

[1] Items deductible for tax purposes but not requiring cash outlays from operations.
[2] Items not deductible for tax purposes requiring cash outlay from operations.
*At the rate for subsidized housing.

You can see that the effect of stabilizing income and expense is to stabilize cash flow. Cash flow is cash generated over and above all cash costs. Cash flow can be distributed to the limited partners and represents another economic benefit. The actual cash loss in the first three years is usually provided, or paid for, by the limited partner capital contribution or the proceeds of the mortgage. This item is referred to as "rent-up loss" — the operating deficit during the period before the property is fully rented. So, the cash flow statement above is not a complete accounting of all the project's sources and uses of funds. It's the income statement used for tax purposes adjusted for items affecting cash flow from operations.

Summary of Benefits

From these financial statements, we can examine three of the four economic benefits of real estate ownership. The bottom line of the first statement shows taxable loss or income. Multiply this figure by your tax bracket, and you can determine your tax savings or tax cost. The cash flow from the second statement represents the cash distributions you will be paid from the property's operations.

The third economic benefit is equity "build-up." This item is the amount of the mortgage you are paying off each year. The "Mortgage Principal Payments" line in the cash flow statement indicates that $236,000 of the mortgage principal is repaid over ten years. So, if the property value merely remains flat with no appreciation, the lender's claim against the property (the un-paid mortgage) goes down from $2,550,000 to $2,314,000. Your equity interest will in effect increase (build-up) by $236,000, from $880,000 to $1,116,000.

The fourth economic benefit is appreciation. Building costs are rising with inflation so it's likely that in ten years the replacement cost of real estate will be much higher than construction costs today. If a property is well located and well maintained, its cash flow should expand over the years and its value increase.

Assume you sell the property in ten years for 25% more than your original cost of $3,430,000 — that's $4,287,500. The quick way to figure your taxable gain is to add up your cumulative tax losses and cash flow — that's $1,699,000. Now, add the cash you'll receive from sale. That's the sale price, $4,287,500, less the mortgage principal amount remaining of $2,314,000, or $1,973,500. The cash from sale, plus the tax losses and cash flow, less your cash investment is the formula for figuring your taxable gain.

Gain On Sale Calculation

Cumulative Tax Loss	$1,354,000
Cumulative Cash Flow	+ 345,000
	1,699,000
Cash From Sale	+ 1,973,500
Less: Cash Investment	− 880,000
Gain on Sale	$2,792,500

A portion of your gain is taxed as ordinary income — the difference between the amount of accelerated depreciation you took and the amount you would have taken if you had used the straight line method. In this case, $413,000 is taxed as ordinary income. The balance is taxed as long term capital gain. In the 50% bracket, your net proceeds after tax will be:

Net Sale Proceeds After Taxes

Sale Price		$4,287,500
Tax Due	50% x $ 413,000 = 206,500	
	20% x $2,379,500 = 475,900	
		− 682,400
Mortgage Repayment		− 2,314,000
Net Proceeds		$1,291,100

To demonstrate the impact of real estate ownership on net worth, you must add up the four economic benefits and compare them to your investment. Cumulative tax losses equal $1,354,000 over the ten year period. In the 50% tax bracket, you'll save $677,000 of taxes you would otherwise pay to the government. Since your cash investment was $880,000, Uncle Sam picks up the tab for 77% of your entire cost. (It is true that, in effect, you pay a tax on these losses when you sell the property. But, the tax is mostly based on favorable capital gains rates.)

The cumulative cash flow equals $345,000 — that is net after-tax dollars in your pocket. So, before equity build-up and appreciation, you've received all your money back plus $142,000 ($677,000 in tax savings plus $345,000 in cumulative cash flow equals $1,022,000; $142,000 more than your $880,000 cash investment).

The calculation of after-tax sale proceeds deducts the paid-down balance of the mortgage. So, the after-tax proceeds of sale, $1,291,100, include equity build-up and appreciation less your tax recapture. Your total return is $677,000 of tax savings, plus $345,000 of cash distributions plus $1,291,100 from the sale — a total of $2,313,100 over ten years on an investment of $880,000. That's with a property appreciation assumption of less than 2.5% per year. Of the total return, 29% comes from tax savings — a source of economic benefits that can only be tapped through direct ownership of assets.

REAL ESTATE: IMPROVED TAX SHELTER UNDER THE NEW TAX LAW

ERTA significantly speeds up depreciation deductions which improves the tax shelter aspects of real estate. (This chapter deals only with non-subsidized residential and commercial property.) Also, the reduced capital gains tax rate and the elimination of the income shifting effects of preference items add shelter benefits to real estate purchase and ownership. Reduced tax brackets cut the new advantage, but most real estate transactions will provide more net benefits for you than before.

Here's the specific impact:

- The improved tax shelter is most striking for commercial property;
- Whatever your tax bracket, you benefit from a higher net present value of tax savings (except for new construction residential property) under the new law. The present value of depreciation deductions is between 19% and 72% higher under the new rules;
- The new benefits are relatively better for existing property than for new property;
- You should probably always use the 15-year straight line method of capital cost recovery for commercial property and the accelerated method for residential property;
- The first 5 years of depreciation are 25% to 109% higher depending on the type of property.

The New Rules

ERTA begins a new system of recovery of capital costs for real property placed in service after 1980. The new system is called the Accelerated Cost Recovery System ("ACRS"). Cost recovery percentages are applied annually to the original cost tax basis of the property. The allowed percentages are either calculated over 15 years on an accelerated basis (the 175% declining balance method switching to straight line to maximize deductions) or are calculated on a straight line basis over 15, 35 or 45 years. The methods for residential and commercial property, new or used, are the same. The cost basis of property is adjusted (reduced) for ACRS deductions in arriving at tax basis to calculate gain or loss on sale.

The first-year recovery percentages are based on the number of months the real estate is owned and in service during the year. Likewise, when the property is sold, the ACRS deduction for the year of disposition reflects the months of the year the property was owned and in service. The applicable cost recovery percentages are in the table on page 183.

For residential property the gain on sale is ordinary income to the extent ACRS deductions exceed the deductions that would have been allowed if the straight line method had been used over a 15-year period (the so-called "recapture" provision). All gain is long-term capital gain for residential property if a straight line method is used.

For non-residential (commercial) property all gain on sale is ordinary income to the extent of all ACRS deductions taken (the same as the rules for personal property). But, if you elect a straight line method for non-residential property, even for the short 15-year period, all gain on sale is capital gain.

The ACRS deductions in excess of deductions that would have been allowed had the 15-year straight line method been used, are items of tax preference. Beginning in 1982, tax preferences no longer reduce the amount of personal service income subject to the 50% maximum tax, because of the reduction in the maximum tax rate to 50%.

Under ACRS, component depreciation is eliminated and composite depreciation is required for the entire building and components (except the personal property portion). For new property, the 15-year depreciable life is generally considerably shorter than the weighted-average useful life reasonably employed under the old law. A further advantage of the new law is the elimination of arguments with the IRS on the amount of allowable depreciation. The ACRS methods are "audit proof" (whichever one you adopt cannot be questioned by the IRS).

The big change in ERTA is the substantial increase in depreciation deductions for purchasing older ("second user") properties. You're allowed the same 15-year ACRS deductions as for new properties. So, you'll have substantially larger depreciation deductions than under the old law.

There are so-called anti-churning rules as well as special transferee rules to prevent you from capitalizing on the new ACRS deductions for property you owned in 1980 or earlier. Situations covered by these rules include sale of property to a related person, like-kind exchanges, "roll-overs" of low income housing and certain sale/leaseback transactions. You are considered related to the previous owner if either one of you own 10% or more commonly in a corporation or partnership; if you are family members; if a common fiduciary relationship exists for both parties; or if there is common control (more than 50% ownership) of the seller and the purchaser. The relationship at the time the property is acquired is what counts. However, if you make a "substantial improvement" to a building, you may use ACRS deductions for the amount of the "substantial improvement." A "substantial improvement" is an expenditure of at least 25% of the adjusted basis of the building (disregarding depreciation) made more than 3 years after the building was placed in service.

In the first five years, the ACRS deductions are 46% of property cost versus a range of 22% to 37%, depending on property type and status under the old law. In fifteen years, 100% of property cost is written off under ACRS versus a range of 60% to 85% under the old law. You can see how depreciation deductions compare under the old and new rules in the table on the following page.

Comparison Of Depreciation Methods

OLD LAW MAXIMUM ALLOWABLE DEPRECIATION

NEW ACRS

NEW CONSTRUCTION | **SECOND USER** | **ALL PROPERTY**

Year	Residential[1]	Commercial[2]	Residential[1]	Commercial[2]	Accelerated	Straight Line
1	8.0%	5.6%	6.6%	4.55%	12%	6.67%
2	7.67	5.2	6.1	4.55	10	6.67
3	7.33	5.0	5.7	4.55	9	6.67
4	7.01	4.7	5.4	4.55	8	6.67
5	6.66	4.4	5.0	4.55	7	6.67
1st Five Years	36.67%	24.9%	28.8%	22.75%	46%	33.35%
6	6.33%	4.2%	5.0%	4.55%	6%	6.67%
7	6.0	3.9	5.0	4.55	6	6.67
8	5.67	3.7	5.0	4.55	6	6.67
9	5.33	3.5	5.0	4.55	6	6.67
10	5.0	3.3	5.0	4.55	5	6.67
2nd Five Years	28.33%	18.6%	25.0%	22.75%	29%	33.35%
11	4.67%	3.3%	5.0%	4.55%	5%	6.66%
12	4.33	3.3	5.0	4.55	5	6.66
13	4.0	3.3	5.0	4.55	5	6.66
14	3.67	3.3	5.0	4.55	5	6.66
15	3.33	3.3	5.0	4.55	5	6.66
3rd Five Years	20.0%	16.5%	25.0%	22.75%	25%	33.30%
1st Fifteen Years	85%	60%	78.8%	68.25%	100%	100%

[1] Arbitrary selection for comparison of twenty-four year sum of years' digits depreciation for new residential. Nineteen year 125% declining balance for used.
[2] Arbitrary selection for comparison of twenty-seven year 150% declining balance depreciation for new commercial. Twenty-two year straight line for used.

The Results

To compare the depreciation deductions under the old and new rules, you can discount the allowable amounts to present value. This method provides an accurate picture of the relative value to you of both systems of depreciation. The table below shows the present value of depreciation per $1,000,000 of asset value for new and second user (existing) residential and commercial properties.

Present Value Of Depreciation
Maximum Allowable

New Property	Old Law	New Law	New Law Straight Line
Residential	$567,700	$675,000	$616,500
Commercial	393,000	675,000	616,500
Second User			
Residential	498,700	675,000	616,500
Commercial	421,700	675,000	616,500

Footnote: Discount rate is 8% for first fifteen years of depreciation. Method of comparison suggested by David Smith of Boston Financial Technology. Weighted-average useful life for residential property of 24 years new and 19 years used. For commercial property, 27 new and 22 years used.

As the table shows, even the new 15-year straight line depreciation gives you substantial additional benefits for all classes of property compared to the old law. The present value of depreciation is dramatically greater (ranging up to a 72% improvement) if you select the new accelerated method.

Now you see how a real estate investment can work and the advantages of the new tax law. We will now show you how to tell whether a particular investment makes good sense or not.

JUDGING VALUE IN REAL ESTATE PRIVATE PLACEMENTS

One way you can judge the economic value of a real estate project before it's built is to look at the permanent mortgage loan commitment. If you know what to look for, you can probably tell both the value of the property and the amount of cash flow you can expect to receive from it. That is likely to be true as long as the mortgage loan is provided by an independent third party such as an insurance company or a savings and loan (an institutional lender, not a governmental or individual lender).

Look at it this way. An insurance company has an objective point of view and is making its own judgment about the value of the property when it offers a loan commitment. Legally, an insurance company mortgage loan can only amount to 75% of property value. That's because an investment that counts toward required reserves is limited to 75% of value (so-called "legal loan to value" ratio). (Some savings and loans may go up to 80% of value). In other words, if an insurance company's appraisal shows the apartment project will be worth $5 million when fully occupied, it can only make a loan for 75% of that amount, or $3,750,000. Knowing this, you can calculate the lender's estimate of future cash flow and property value.

Mortgage loans are typically secured by the property, the so-called non-recourse loans. In the event that interest and principal aren't paid on time, the lender can only take possession of the property. He cannot pursue the individuals or partnerships that are involved. As a result, the process of determining property value is very important to the institutional mortgage lender. He only has recourse to the property and its value for repayment of his loan.

The institutional lender obtains a property valuation (appraisal) when determining whether or not to make the mortgage loan. The appraised value is the theoretical transaction price a willing buyer would pay a willing seller, each knowing the relevant facts.

Usually, appraised value is determined by blending the results of three methods of analysis — replacement cost, recent transaction prices for comparable properties (market approach), and the present value of the stream of income the property will throw off over its useful economic life (the income method). Normally, the income method is given more weight. (Note: Tax shelter losses are not considered a factor in determining property value.)

Try to determine the value of the property yourself — if you're convinced the deal and the people involved are sound. At the very least, going through the exercise we suggest below will provide you with some interesting questions to ask the person who's selling the deal. Sometimes comparing the insurance company's numbers with the number in the offering memorandum can be a real eye-opener.

The Calculation of Value

In order to find out what the mortgage lender thinks the property is worth, divide the mortgage loan amount by .75.

.75 x Property Value = Mortgage Loan Amount

Property Value = $\dfrac{\text{Mortgage Loan Amount}}{.75}$

Dividing a $3,750,000 mortgage loan by .75 gives a total property value of $5,000,000. That means the equity value is $1,250,000 according to the mortgage lender — that's the total property value of $5,000,000 minus the mortgage loan of $3,750,000. (Technically, for sake of simplicity, this procedure assumes that the "capitalization rate," explained later, for the debt portion and the equity portion of property value is the same.)

So, if you're asked to put up more cash than $1,250,000, you're paying more than the mortgage lender thinks it's worth. That's also true if you put up $1,250,000 but you (the limited partners as a group) buy less than 100% of the property. That can happen if, at the partnership level, the limited partner/investor won't own 100% of the partnership's interest in the property. Instead, you might share some of the economic benefits (cash flow or refinancing and sale proceeds) with the general partner.

When you determine the amount of cash you put up, add in everything (including interest required on future payment obligations) regardless of how the offering memorandum says the money will be spent. Don't just look at the portion of your cash investment that the offering document earmarks for the property. That's because you'll want to recover all the cash you put up, not just a portion of it, when you sell the property.

Even paying a little more for the property can add significantly to your equity investment. For instance, if you pay $5,625,000 instead of $5,000,000, that's an increase of 12.5%. But, you'd be putting up an extra $625,000 above the $1,250,000 equity value. Therefore, you're paying 50% more than the lender's assessment of the equity value of the property.

The Calculation of Cash Flow

You can also determine what the lender thinks the cash flow of the property will be. Remember, for the lender the income method is the most important one for determining value.

The lender calculates rents (income) and operating costs (expenses) to determine the net operating income from the property, because it's the net operating income that will repay the interest and principal (debt service) on the mortgage loan. The net operating income is the cash the property would generate if it were free and clear of mortgage debt.

The lender only uses 75% of the net to pay debt service on his loan. (That's another way to show that the loan is 75% of the value.) So, if you divide the annual debt service (interest plus principal payments) by .75 you can determine the net cash flow (net operating income) the lender thinks the property will generate. That formula is shown on the following page.

(Sometimes 80% of cash flow will be required to cover debt service, so you might want to calculate the numbers using the 80% figure too.)

$$.75 \times \text{Cash Flow} = \text{Debt Service}$$

$$\text{Cash Flow} = \frac{\text{Debt Service}}{.75}$$

Here's how it might work. Assume the debt service cost would be about 10.8% for a loan on an apartment project, or $405,000 on a $3,750,000 mortgage loan. The net cash flow expected by the lender would be $540,000 ($405,000 divided by .75). So, $135,000 ($540,000 minus $405,000) is the cash flow after debt service. In other words, if everything goes according to projection, you'll receive a 10.8% return on your cash investment ($135,000 divided by $1,250,000) assuming you own 100% of the property.

Now compare the lender's estimate of cash flow from this calculation with the estimate in the projections you're given. Usually, the projections in the offering memorandum will show a higher figure.

The lender's view is usually more conservative (indicating lower property value) than the developer's or the syndicator's and maybe even the market's view. More than likely, that's because of high interest rates, tight money and the lender's caution stemming from memories of the problems that arose in the real estate industry in the middle 70's. Certainly, you should be able to justify to your satisfaction any discrepancy between the lender's view and the view expressed in the offering memorandum.

In Perspective

In general, we don't think you should ever pay more than the property value derived from these calculations. First, the limited partners won't own 100% of the property because of the general partner's share.

Second, you're buying based on a pro forma income statement — an estimate of what the future may bring two or three years from the time you make your investment. There is risk the expected results won't appear. That might be all right if you could have a cash flow guarantee — but you can't, at least not from a reputable source. You might arrange for an adjustment in price from the seller if the property doesn't measure up, but it's unlikely. A third alternative is to arrange that some of the cash you invest remain as a contingency reserve or as working capital.

Of course, our mortgage valuation method is not foolproof for many important reasons. Often the lender does a lot of business with a particular developer and the loan amount may not be an objective measure of value. Sometimes lenders are very aggressive in putting out mortgage money — as they were during 1971 and 1972. Consequently, the value calculation we suggest could result in a higher equity value than would make sense.

If you become involved in real estate investments, you are bound to hear the term capitalization rate. The overall capitalization rate is the yield of the property — the annual net cash flow (net operating income) divided by the sale price or estimate of value. In the valuation example above we valued the property at an overall capitalization rate which equaled the mortgage constant (debt service divided by the loan amount).

$$\text{Capitalization Rate} = \frac{\text{Net Operating Income}}{\text{Property Value}}$$

Buyers of real estate today will accept a lower return (yield) on the cash portion of purchase price (equity) than mortgage lenders will accept on the debt portion. Ten percent returns on equity are high today. But, you can calculate the amount you could pay for the property in our example and receive an 8% return. Here's how:

$$\frac{\text{Cash Flow}}{\text{Equity Return}} = \frac{\$135,000}{.08} = \$1,687,500$$

Another Way To Judge Value

Besides looking at the mortgage loan, there is another way you can determine whether the price is right in an apartment syndication for new construction. Calculate total construction costs, operating and fixed expenses and rents per apartment unit, and check them locally. It's easier than you'd think.

The first step is to calculate the total cost per unit in the project. You can do that by adding the amount of money the limited partners put up and the principal amount of any permanent mortgage loans on the project. This is the total cost. Now divide by the number of apartment units to give you the cost per unit. You will be able to compare this figure with other local projects. Example:

Limited Partner Capital Contribution	$1,687,500
Permanent Mortgage	+ 3,750,000
Total Cost	$5,437,500
Number of Apartment Units	÷ 218
Cost Per Unit	$25,000

Now look at property expenses. Major expenses consist of operating costs and local real estate taxes. Operating costs include utilities, maintenance and repairs, insurance, security, snow and trash removal, legal and accounting, management payroll and fees, etc. First, take these figures from the financial projections.

Add up all the operating expenses and taxes, and then calculate total costs on a per unit basis. Be careful not to include syndication costs and fees payable to the builder or general partner. These are usually paid out of your capital contribution and are not property operating expenses.

Assuming the tenant pays his own heat and electric, you'll find that operating expenses and taxes per apartment unit generally run $1300 to $1400 per year. But, there are wide variations in operating costs in different parts of the country.

For instance, real estate taxes may vary from 20% to 40% of total costs, etc.

In more normal financial markets than we have experienced recently, interest and principal payments on the mortgage would likely be about 11% ($412,500 a year on a $3,750,000 mortgage) or $1,892 per apartment unit. Now assume that you will want to make 8% per year on your cash investment of $1,687,500 or $135,000 ($619 per apartment unit).

Now add up the various expenses and your desired equity return:

	Per Unit
Equity Return	$619
Mortgage Payments	+ 1,892
Operating Expenses and Taxes	+ 1,400
Total	$3,911
Vacancy Factor (1)	÷ .95
Rent Per Year	$4,117
Required Monthly Rent (÷ 12)	$343

(1) The vacancy factor adjustment is necessary because the property will not always be full. We used 5% here as a vacancy provision. It may be higher in some areas.

You just calculated the level of rent necessary for this project to be economically viable — to pay its costs and provide a minimum return on investment.

Now you have assembled the information you need to begin your personal check on the figures you've been given:

- Construction Cost
- Operating Cost
- Taxes
- Rents

It's important to confirm these figures with local sources. We suggest the first place to start is with local lending institutions, such as savings and loans and banks. You should also call the project's actual lender. And, you can try the Chamber of Commerce and township officials such as the engineer, building inspector and tax assessor. After all, they have an interest in boosting the local economy and your investment will help.

Many banks make what are called construction loans. These are mortgages on property which is in the process of being built as distinguished from permanent mortgages which are loans on completed property. Construction lenders will be familiar with costs in the local area for the kind of property you're considering.

Sometimes construction costs are measured in cost per square foot. This is a much more accurate measure of construction cost than the cost per apartment unit. That's because apartment size can vary considerably. This may mean that you have to make one extra calculation to compare figures from local sources with figures in the offering memo. But, be sure to use figures on projects that are truly comparable. The variables include location, construction standards, property type, size and amenities such as swimming pool, tennis courts, sauna, etc.

There are other ways to check out local construction costs and rent levels. Some data is published on the subject. Here is some guidance about how to calculate costs per square foot of building from information available in mid-1981. Included are representative costs in various areas for several types of buildings.

Remember, the starting point is the cost of the building you are investing in. Add all the limited partners' cash contributions to all the debt — that's the purchase price of the property. (Be sure if you're buying a fractional interest, you "gross up" the price to 100%.) Divide the purchase price by the square feet of the building and you have the total purchase price (or cost) per square foot. Now compare your costs with the representative cost figures given in the tables on pages 106 through 108. The tables show costs for apartments, office buildings and shopping centers. General figures of this type are nothing more than a rough guide, but they can improve your investment decision-making process.

The data for current construction costs and rents for fifteen major real estate markets was compiled and published in the Eton Journal, "Data Tables: A Reference for Real

Estate Decision," March - April 1981. Costs for "city" construction reflect high-rise structures whereas "suburban" construction is low-rise or garden type. High-rise construction costs are at least 30% more than low-rise construction costs. In general, city rents are higher reflecting additional construction costs. The construction costs presented are for the buildings, including construction loan interest. Land costs, working capital for rent-up period losses, developer overhead and demolition costs are not included. So, total construction costs could well be 25% greater than shown.

The key, of course, is rent (or lease rate). If costs for new construction in your deal are much higher than in these tables, you'd better be able to charge commensurately higher rents. You can also use these tables for rough comparison when buying existing buildings. Usually existing properties sell at a 20%-25% discount, or more, from new construction costs.

Rents are the hardest thing of all to accurately forecast. You need to know the condition of the local market — comparable rents, vacancy rates and prospects for new construction that may be competitive with your project.

In our example on page 103, we determined the rent level necessary for the project to be economically viable. To check out the project, try this figure out on those you call. Remember, new apartment projects will generally rent for more than old apartments, especially in an active rental property area. The new appliances, carpets and condition of the buildings have a certain appeal.

Using this technique should enable you to weed out the really bad deal. If your survey is satisfactory, you'll proceed with the investment with more confidence. And, we doubt these calls and calculations will take too much of your time.

By the way, the local reputation and track record of the developer are very important considerations. So, don't hesitate to make adequate inquiries about him and his company. You may learn some interesting things. Try to look at other projects which he has built. Were there construction problems? Are the properties well maintained and well rented? Are his bills paid on time?

Apartment Buildings*

	CITY			SUBURBAN		
	Vacancy Rate (1)	Const. Cost (2)	Rental Rate (3)	Vacancy Rate (1)	Const. Cost (2)	Rental Rate (3)
Atlanta	1%	N.C.	$ 425	4%	$24	$355
Boston	2	$60	670	4	50	500
Chicago	2	50	650	6	48	430
Dallas	1	53**	420	4	28	400
Denver	1	57	395	2	40	328
Houston	3	28**	365	6	25	330
Kansas City, MO	4	65	535	6	38	350
Los Angeles	3	44	430	4	41	410
Miami	1	N.C.	600	1	26	400
New York	1	80	1,200	1	50	663
Phoenix	8	N.C.	430	6	26	363
Pittsburgh	1	37**	675	1	29**	388
San Diego	2	43	400	2	40	485
San Francisco	1	88	900	2	75	525
Wash., D.C.	1	60	600	2	50	500
AVERAGE		$55	$ 580		$39	$428

(1) Percentage of units empty.
(2) New construction cost per square foot.
(3) Per unit per month, unfurnished, one-year lease, with heat and hot water, without electricity.

N.C. - No new construction during period.

* Data is for December 1980, based on a new two bedroom unit of 900-950 square feet as follows: City - high-rise, elevator, 200-300 units; Suburban - garden type, 100-150 units with pool and tennis.
**Data for June 1980.

Shopping Centers*

	REGIONAL Vacancy Rate (1)	REGIONAL Const. Cost (2)	REGIONAL Lease Rate (3)	COMMUNITY Vacancy Rate (1)	COMMUNITY Const. Cost (2)	COMMUNITY Lease Rate (3)
Atlanta	3%	$53	$13	3%	$27	$6
Boston	1	66	16	5	31	5
Chicago	1	41	20	5	36	7
Dallas	4	40	15	8	35	7
Denver	1	47	22	4	39	6
Houston	8	38	12	4	35	6
Kansas City, MO	5	33	14	6	33	6
Los Angeles	2	49	9	5	71	9
Miami	2	N.C.	12	3	33	5
New York	2	57	17	2	45	9
Phoenix	3	50	17	7	29	5
Pittsburgh	1	45**	25	1	30**	5
San Diego	2	48	8	5	71	8
San Francisco	1	85	23	8	31	6
Wash., D.C.	10	55	17	8	35	5
AVERAGE		$51	$16		$39	$6

(1) Percentage empty.
(2) New construction cost per square foot including mall (buildings), parking lot and common areas (not land).
(3) Gross lease rate per square foot per year, for minor (not anchor) tenants in regionals and for anchors in community centers, excluding percentage rents (typically an additional 1% to 3% of gross sales) and common area charges and maintenance, but including insurance, property tax and operating cost pass-throughs.

N.C. - No new construction during period.

* Data is for December 1980, based on: Regional - 500,000 to 1,000,000 square foot enclosed malls; Community - 100,000 to 500,000 square foot unenclosed centers.
**Data for August 1980.

Office Buildings*

	CITY			SUBURBAN		
	Vacancy Rate (1)	Const. Cost (2)	Lease Rate (3)	Vacancy Rate (1)	Const. Cost (2)	Lease Rate (3)
Atlanta	11%	$51	$15	8%	$45	$11
Boston	1	90	21	4	55	15
Chicago	4	53	18	16	45	14
Dallas	4	55	13	7	48	11
Denver	2	58	18	7	51	14
Houston	4	68	18	9	48	13
Kansas City, MO	9	63	10	6	55	11
Los Angeles	2	66	23	2	56	18
Miami	3	53	18	4	48	19
New York	4	88	28	4	62	17
Phoenix	9	65	14	9	40	14
Pittsburgh	1	80	18	3	50	12
San Diego	4	66	14	4	56	10
San Francisco	1	95	20	7	83	18
Wash., D.C.	1	60	20	3	48	14
AVERAGE		$67	$18		$53	$14

(1) Percentage empty.
(2) New construction cost per square foot for building and site work, excluding land, architectural and demolition cost and pre-opening overhead.
(3) Gross lease rate per square foot per year, with escalation.

* Data is for December 1980, based on prime office buildings as follows: City - 350,000 to 500,000 square feet (20 or 30 stories); Suburban - 100,000 square feet (5 stories or less).

INVESTING IN PUBLIC
REAL ESTATE PARTNERSHIPS

Let's assume you're convinced that real estate values will rise and you want to take advantage of it by putting more of your net worth in assets which may appreciate. You know what's happened to the equity value of your house. It's increased dramatically. At the same time, you've seen how leverage can work to your advantage. Still, you're not in the $500,000 plus net worth category, so you're not able to make a large investment in a single real estate private placement. And, you don't have the time to become involved in day-to-day property management or the selection of a choice local real estate investment.

You're just like fifty thousand other investors who turned to publicly registered real estate partnerships last year and put up $5,000 or more for an interest in a diversified property portfolio.

You can choose between partnerships that invest in apartments, net leases or commercial properties. Some partnerships buy properties while they're still under construction or before they're proven to be economically viable. These offer the largest tax shelter losses which can be used to offset income from other sources. And, some partnerships buy completed properties with existing tenants. These provide cash flow right from the start. Each investment will provide a different return, and each will have a different level of economic risk. From among those offered, how do you select the particular investment medium that's right for you? First learn to differentiate the risks.

Real Estate Risks

In any real estate development, there are three periods of risk. The first is the construction period — the time before the property is ready for occupancy. Obvious risks during this period include the possibility of major problems in completing the building (the contractor might go broke first); of actual building costs exceeding budget (inflation may throw estimates out of whack); of construction delays (due to strikes, material shortages, etc.). These factors are all beyond control and would increase interest charges or result in possible loss of the permanent mortgage commitment if the building isn't completed on time. They could even result in bankruptcy of the project.

The second risk period occurs after completion of construction but before substantial occupancy. This is the so-called rent-up period. Here you'll find out whether you have a good location; whether the rents you projected are realistic; whether you can hold the line on operating costs; whether you have enough money to see the project through to substantial occupancy; and, finally, whether you built the right type of property.

The final risk period is the operational period — the time between completion of rent-up and the ultimate sale of the property. During this period, you have to negotiate with tenants and determine lease terms and rents; decide on repairs and improvements to remain competitive with new construction; maximize your return through effective management; and perhaps, most importantly, you have to figure out when to sell or refinance the property.

The more of these risks you assume, the higher the return you should expect on your investment. But, there are other factors that affect your return — principally the intended use of the property and the contractual relationship you have with the tenants.

Put simply, real estate tends to sell on the basis of the security and characteristics of its income stream — the credit of the tenants and the length and terms of their leases. Let's examine the different types of property, categorizing the return on each by the specific type of tenancy.

Assume you rent an entire building for twenty-five years to General Motors which absolutely agrees to pay all operating and maintenance costs (a net lease). You won't receive a high return because you have very little risk. But, the return you do receive will be very secure.

Now consider a shopping center. Normally, a substantial portion (say 60%) will be rented to larger store chains (J.C. Penney, Sears, etc.) on long-term leases, 25 years or more. But smaller operations, such as restaurants and pet shops, will probably fill out the tenant roster, usually on five year (or shorter) leases. As the owner, you'll have to pay certain operating expenses. So, a shopping center is a little more risky than the net lease discussed above, and you should receive a higher return.

Office buildings tend to have a mixture of large and small tenants with predominantly five and ten year leases. Here we have shorter leases and less substantial tenants. And, you can't always pass along cost increases to your tenants. As a rule, you will pay a lower multiple of income for an office building than for a shopping center — which means your cash return as owner should be somewhat higher.

Apartments are usually rented for short periods, say one year or less, and credit problems with tenants will invariably arise. So again, your cash return should be higher than for office buildings and shopping centers.

Finally, hotels re-rent all the rooms every few nights. Therefore, hotels should provide the highest yield of all because the tenancy is very uncertain.

Note: Real estate (especially completed property) usually sells on a yield basis — the cash flow you receive annually compared with your cash investment. This is known as the cash-on-cash return (equivalent to yield for a security). Tax shelter losses aren't really a factor in evaluation.

The Right Investment For You

Now let's assume you're looking for a safe real estate investment. You want inflation protection without much risk. And, you want some income on your investment from the start. A real estate partnership which buys completed commercial properties, such as shopping centers and office buildings, should fit you perfectly. Here's why.

Since the buildings are up and running, there's no construction or rent-up risk. The credit of the tenants is good and the leases are long. That puts you at the lower end of the risk spectrum.

And, you'll have a historical perspective on the property's income and expenses. So, the tax losses (accounting characteristics) and the cash flow are going to be fairly predictable. (One note of caution: Some partnerships buy properties still under construction on terms to complete payment when the building is up and operating. However, you are still taking on additional risks compared to buying completed properties.)

With this type of completed commercial property investment, you should receive a return of 6% to 7% a year after tax during the first five or six years which derives from a combination of tax savings and cash distributions. The projected benefits during the first six years of ownership are shown below:

$10,000 Commercial Property Investment
Initial Ownership Phase

Year	Taxable Income (Loss)	A Tax Savings	B Cash Flow	A+B Economic Benefits After Tax
1982*	($400)	$200	$600	$800
1983	(300)	150	600	750
1984	(300)	150	600	750
1985	(200)	100	650	750
1986	(100)	50	700	750
1987	—	—	750	750

*Assumes a full year of investment and tax savings in the 50% tax bracket.

After six years or so, the partnership may begin liquidating by selling off properties. Let's assume your equity in the properties appreciates at 6% a year. To see how you'll make out, we assumed the partnership would sell 10% of the properties each year from 1989 through 1993 and liquidate the rest of the properties at the end of 1994. These results are shown in the table below.

**$10,000 Commercial Property Investment
Liquidation Phase**

Year	A Net Cash Flow After Tax	B Sales Proceeds After Tax	A+B Economic Benefits After Tax
1988	$800	—	$ 800
1989	700	$1304	2004
1990	600	1366	1966
1991	500	1434	1934
1992	450	1508	1958
1993	355	1589	1944
1994	250	7672	7922

Note: Assumes a 50% tax rate for Net Cash Flow and a 20% capital gains tax rate for Sale Proceeds.

If we add up the after-tax economic benefits each year at 6% compound interest (this assumes you can reinvest at this rate after tax), you will accumulate total benefits after tax of $26,363 in the 50% bracket on your original $10,000 investment.

Projecting 6% price appreciation on your equity investment could very easily be too conservative. The reason: The total value of the property is much larger than your equity investment. Each property is mortgaged. It's just like your house - if your equity is $25,000, the market value could be $100,000 and you may be borrowing $75,000. In our example, we projected 6% appreciation on $25,000 of equity. If we instead projected 6% appreciation on property value of $100,000 (much more realistic), your rate of return would be about twice as high.

In this kind of investment, you're not taking much risk if the partnership you select is large enough to diversify over several properties, and management has a good track record. If the partnership raises $15-$20 million of equity (limited partner capital contributions), it will be able to purchase $50-$60 million of properties by financing with mortgages.

Another important consideration with real estate in general is that real estate requires staying power. Staying power is especially important if you're investing in new construction because in recessions, or in periods of high interest rates, conditions are difficult for new construction. It's the classic time for trouble.

You must select a sponsor that has good relationships with mortgage lenders and good banking connections. He should have a substantial net worth and have made it through tough times intact. Even good properties can experience problems due to competition and other factors. You need a sponsor with staying power.

Finally, real estate is hard to buy well. Just because you have the cash, doesn't mean you can make a good deal. Good properties are hard to find at the right price. So, if a sponsor invested $30 million last year and wants to invest $100 million this year, he probably can't — wisely. And, you shouldn't back him. Stick with someone who has consistently done the job and who isn't trying to own the world. That's the best way to insure a successful investment.

Investor Costs

Investor costs in public deals look high, but they probably aren't. The up-front costs are about the same when you buy a house as they are for a public real estate partnership that uses borrowed funds to buy properties. If you pay a 6% real estate brokerage commission on a $100,000 house, that's $6,000. You would probably borrow $75,000 and put up $25,000 of cash to buy it. So, the $6,000 commission, plus perhaps $1,000 more in closing costs, equals $7,000, or 28% of your $25,000 cash down payment.

In any event, there's not much variation in fees charged among the larger partnerships. Costs paid by the partnership out of initial capital may be as high as 30% of the amount you put up (so-called up-front costs). About one-third goes to the stockbroker, one-third to the program sponsor and one-third to unaffiliated real estate brokers.

In addition, the sponsor will receive compensation during partnership operations — 10% of the cash distributions, but usually only after your return reaches a specified level, say at least 6% on your original investment.

The partnership will probably wind up in ten or twelve years by selling all properties and distributing the cash. First, you receive your original investment plus say a 6% cumulative return. Then the sponsor receives a real estate commission usually equal to one-half the amount he earned up front. If there is any excess cash available, usually 85% goes to you and 15% to the sponsor. It's important that the sponsor receives these payments both during the operating period as well as in liquidation. This type of arrangement will keep the sponsor's interests focused and closely aligned with your own.

Unless you are wealthy and knowledgeable enough to pursue your own property acquisition program, your best bet is to buy into one of the larger real estate income partnerships. You can take advantage of the buying opportunity the present state of economy has provided and buy diversification of your investment as well. These partnerships are offered by investment program sponsors described as "syndicators." Dealing with them makes sense.

Here are the reasons the national real estate partnerships are good investment vehicles:

- A National View - Demographics, energy considerations, population shifts, patterns of economic development and political environments are all important considerations in real estate investing. The individual developer is usually bound by the confines of a fairly modest geographical area and short-run considerations. The big real estate buyer can select those areas of the country he deems best.
- Investment Strategy - The major real estate partnerships can articulate an acquisition philosophy and execute purchases to take advantage of shorter-term market trends. For instance, regions and areas become overbuilt for certain kinds of properties, temporarily depressing rents and prices. Some partnerships specialize in this type of depressed price acquisition. Prices for properties can vary considerably between regions and be-

tween primary and secondary cities. Perhaps the right approach is to buy only in the relatively lower-priced areas. Also, the large real estate buyer can set a mix of properties in a portfolio to reflect different combinations of predictable current income and upside potential.

- Acquisition Talent - The selection of properties is a demanding job requiring an interesting blend of analytical, negotiating and entrepreneurial skills. Acquisition personnel usually earn performance compensation and status as principals of the company. Exposure to a multitude of acquisition prospects and developers improves knowledge of the market.

- Triple-A Properties - At today's costs, major properties in good locations with prime tenants can cost $25 to $50 million or more. In the real estate business, size and prime location are key ingredients for long-term investment success. About the only way most people can participate in owning this top quality grade of commercial real estate today is in a group with other investors.

- Diversification - The performance of a pool of properties over the long run is much easier to predict than the fortunes of any single building. The phrase "staying power" means having cash flow, borrowing capability and management talent to weather the inevitable problems a particular property may encounter. Staying power comes in part from a diversified portfolio.

- Financing Sophistication - The smart buyer can accomplish important objectives for the seller in structuring transactions and that can make the deal fly. With mortgage money expensive and/or unavailable, sophisticated financing alternatives can make or break a deal. In today's tough lending environment, large active real estate buyers can utilize bank lines and financing sources that may be unavailable to smaller companies.

- Management - In the physical operation, maintenance and repair of properties, a large company can have experts in-house and benefit from volume purchases at lower costs for items like carpets and appliances. Operating large numbers of properties with the use of sophisticated accounting controls and management information systems can improve efficiency and create value by increasing cash flow.

- Maximize Value - A large diversified real estate partnership can be a "strong seller". Since these partnerships are designed to liquidate out, they are a visable source of properties that buyers seek out. Management's knowledge of markets may enable them to sell at top dollar. And, financial sophistication and good property management will also help achieve above-average results from sales.

- Batting Average - Partnerships formed in the early 70's have been liquidated out at gains of three to five times original investment and more. No serious financial problems were encountered by the large national real estate partnerships even through the real estate "depression" of 1974-1976. Investment results that were advertised have largely been achieved.

- Liquidity - Most large brokerage firms "accommodate" clients in finding a market for limited partnership units if you want to sell. An NASD committee is reviewing the idea of establishing a secondary market for limited partnership units in publicly registered deals. And, liquidity comes from partial liquidation and payout of capital gains as well. Any similar level of liquidity is difficult to achieve in private placements.

- Disclosure - Offering documents are subject to close scrutiny and often independent consultants execute due diligence or feasibility study assignments on the sponsors and the offerings. Investor reporting and investor services departments are generally good.

- Availability - Primarily due to a lack of new construction, these partnerships are about the only game in town for those interested in purchasing real estate. Also, achieving proper diversification by investing in a series of private placements might require $250,000 or more, well beyond the range of most investors.

APARTMENTS AS INVESTMENTS

The hot spot in real estate in the early 80's is apartments. The prices of apartment projects and apartment rents will probably rise because the stock of rental apartments has declined dramatically while the demand has increased substantially. Demographic trends and the affordability of single family residential housing also indicate tremendous future demand for rental apartments.

In most of the 70's, the market was working off the glut or over-building of apartments that occurred in the early 70's. But now, there is no excess supply of rental apartments, rather there is a shortage. Vacancy rates were typically in excess of 10% then. Now, vacancy rates are about 5%, considered by most to be the practical minimum in the management of an apartment project.

In fact, apartment rents have recently begun to increase faster than the Consumer Price Index after lagging behind for most of the decade of the 70's. One reason rents are low is that historically the housing industry has had access to inexpensive credit from savings and loans. So, the portion of cost represented by debt service was artificially low. For another, the rising price of single family homes meant single family homes were very competitive relative to apartments from the standpoint of their real cost of occupancy (costs less appreciation). This held apartment rents down.

The noted real estate economist, Anthony Downs of the Brookings Institution, now predicts apartment rents will rise faster than the CPI in 1982 and the foreseeable future. The reasons: Today's expensive borrowing has to be reflected in rent levels; house prices won't keep rising as fast as they have; apartment rents are a bargain now; and supply-demand factors are exerting strong upward pressure on rents. This outlook for rising rental rates is bullish for apartment investments because, all other things equal, rising rents mean rising property values.

Supply Factors

The squeeze on the entire residential housing stock has resulted in the lowest vacancy rates for apartments and rental housing since the Second World War. Here's why. Since 1975, the population has grown 16.8 million, or 7.9%. Households have increased 9.3 million, or 13.1%. During the same period, the net addition to dwelling units was only 2.8 million, or 3.4%. In addition, the Reagan Administration is trying to kill federal housing construction and mortgage subsidies. These current policies are likely to substantially reduce the government-assisted addition to the housing stock in 1983 and thereafter, reducing the potential supply of new units. This will also pave the way for higher rents because government housing is generally low-rent housing.

The specific outlook for rental apartments may be even more striking than for all residential housing. Apartment starts since 1975 totalled 3,286,000 units. The guess is that approximately 1,676,000 of those units were either apartments constructed for sale as condominiums or condominium conversions of existing apartments, which removes those units from the stock of rental apartments.

In addition to the condominium craze, apartment units are lost from the rental housing stock through destruction and uninhabitability (called "disappearances"). The number of these disappearances probably totals about 2,278,000 units since 1974.

Including condominium construction and conversion and probable apartment disappearances from 1974 through 1981, the stock of rental apartments actually declined by 673,000 units. In the last three years alone, the reduction in rental apartments nationwide was 468,000 units.

The underproduction of private apartments (total apartment starts less public housing and government subsidized housing) is even more dramatic. The probable net reduction in the private apartment stock is 947,000 units since 1974 and 650,000 units in the last three years alone. The following tables tell the story:

Apartment Housing — Total
(000's)

	1975	1976	1977	1978	1979	1980	1981	Cumulative 1975-1981
Total Multi-Family Starts (1)	279	432	551	603	566	460	395	3,286
Less: Condo Starts and Conversions	-114	-165	-205	-272	-343	-316	-266	-1,681
Addition to Apartment Stock (2)	165	267	346	331	223	144	129	1,605
Less: Disappearances	-363	-304	-335	-312	-320	-322	-322	-2,278
Net Addition (Reduction) To Apartment Stock	(198)	(37)	11	19	(97)	(178)	(193)	(673)

(1) Source: Bureau of Census and HUD.
(2) Source: 1979 and 1980 Advance Mortgage. Other years Robert A. Stanger & Co. estimate.

Apartment Housing Stock - Private
(000's)

	1975	1976	1977	1978	1979	1980	1981	Cumulative 1975-1981
Conventional Multi-Family Starts (1)	246	356	403	414	383	294	302	2,398
Less: Condo Starts and Conversions (2)	-114	-165	-205	-272	-343	-316	-266	-1,681
Addition (Reduction) to Private Apartment Stock	132	191	198	142	40	(22)	36	717
Less: Disappearances (3)	-265	-222	-245	-228	-234	-235	-235	-1,664
Net Addition (Reduction) Private Apartment Starts	(133)	(31)	(47)	(86)	(194)	(257)	(199)	(947)

(1) Total apartment starts less public housing and government subsidized housing. Source: Bureau of Census and HUD.
(2) Assumes no subsidized housing conversions.
(3) 73% of total Disappearances, the ratio of private starts to total starts.

Demand Factors

The demand side of the equation seems bullish also. The increase in the number of households in the last seven years implies the need for 2,188,000 apartment units. That's because occupied apartments have historically been 23% of total households and households have grown by 9.3 million since 1975. The shortfall in new construction is then 2,861,000 units, the number required by household formations plus the net reduction in the rental apartment stock of 673,000 units. The current stock of rental housing is estimated at approximately 19.6 million units, so the 2.9 million unit shortfall amounts to a very substantial 14.8% of total rental housing.

But the outlook for continuing apartment demand is the subject of a certain amount of controversy. On the one hand are the views on household formations offered by Professor Dwight Jaffee, specialist in real estate finance at Princeton University. The number of households grew almost half again as fast as the population from 1976 through 1981, and he views the reduction in the number of people per household as a trend that's likely to continue. According to Jaffee, there is another factor in the demand for housing. "The baby boom is finally upon us," he says, pointing out that the last of that birth period is considered to be 1960. "There are going to be a great many new households formed between now and 1986. Five years worth of 25-year olds will be coming into the market by 1986 with no place to live."

On the other hand, the New York City-based economic and investment counselors, Siff, Oakley and Marks, Inc., suggest a different shape for the demand for housing. They point out that the number of people age 18 through 34 will not increase during the next decade. This age group comprises the bulk of new household formations. So, this base component of household formations will be static. Most of the growth will have to come from the continuation of the non-traditional sources of formations such as individuals living alone, single parent households and older folks deciding to maintain their independence.

While household formations will certainly affect the outlook for residential housing, the greatest stimulus to the continuing demand for apartments will be the "affordability gap" relative to single family houses. (See the table on the next page.)

Single family housing prices and carrying costs appear to have pushed most people out of the market. Carrying costs have tripled while incomes have doubled since 1974. This fact will postpone the age at which first ownership occurs and might even alter the nature of first ownership from a single family detached unit to some form of cluster townhouse or condominium ownership. This will increase the demand for rental apartments and accelerate the conversion of rental units to condominiums, increasing the scarcity of those few rental units remaining.

The Outlook for Rent Levels

Apartment rents rose at a 6% annual rate from 1970 through 1977 and at an 8% rate from 1978 through 1980. The increase in 1981 was 8.9%, higher than the CPI for the first time in many years.

One way to evaluate the upside potential for apartment rents is to look at the high cost of debt today. This high cost must be built into rent levels or new projects won't be built. The implication for rents on existing properties is for substantial increases. For instance, an apartment project carrying a mortgage loan equal to 70% of its cost will require rents that are 22% higher at a 16% mortgage rate than at a 10% rate.

Another way to measure the upside potential in rents is to compare average rents with rents necessary to pay a fair return on today's construction costs for bricks and mortar. In 1974, apartment rents nationwide averaged 20 cents per square foot per month. At construction costs and borrowing rates prevailing at the time, rents of 28 cents per square foot per month were necessary to make projects economic. The spread was 8 cents. So new construction rents needed to be 40% above prevailing rents to make new construction "pencil out."

Today, average rents are approximately 36 cents per square foot per month. Rents necessary to justify new apartment construction are in the neighborhood of 65 cents per

Single-Family Home Mortgage Costs Vs. "Young Family" Income
(Year of Purchase)

Year	Average Selling Price*	Average Amount Financed*	Average Initial Rate*	Average Term* (yrs.)	First-Year Payments Interest	First-Year Payments Principal	First-Year Payments Total	"Young Family" Income**	Average Payments as % of Income
1974	$35,700	$26,100	8.99	23.6	$2,346	$354	$2,700	$12,354	21.9%
1976	44,000	31,700	9.08	25.1	2,879	366	3,245	14,440	22.5
1978	56,800	41,200	9.56	26.7	3,939	377	4,316	16,949	25.5
1979	68,000	48,300	10.87	27.4	5,250	330	5,580	18,932	29.5
1980	73,400	51,600	12.86	27.2	6,635	257	6,892	19,977	34.5
1981	76,500	53,700	14.99	26.4	8,050	206	8,256	21,150	39.0
					Forecast				
1982	78,000	54,600	15.00	26.8	8,190	198	8,388	22,450	37.4

Source: Courtesy of Siff, Oakley & Marks.

* Federal Home Loan Bank Board (Notes: Average selling price, amount financed, rate and term refer to a weighted average of new and existing home sales made via conventional mortgages. Rate refers to "effective" rate, including contract interest rate and fees.)
** Department of Commerce, Bureau of the Census. (Note: Average Family Income of families headed by individuals under 35 years of age.)

square foot per month. The spread is 29 cents which means that rents for new construction need to be 81% above prevailing rents.

Looking at it the other way around, average apartment rents can almost double before they approach the umbrella, or ceiling, represented by rent levels for new apartment projects. The other implication is that there will be little new apartment construction (except in selected markets) unless prevailing rental rates rise. From 1971 to 1981, average apartment rents rose 80%, and apartment project prices doubled. The outlook seems better now than ever before.

By comparison, average office space rents rose 15% in 1979, 18% in 1980 and 26% in 1981. Commensurately, office construction put in place in dollars was up 28% in 1981 and will probably rise at a faster rate both in 1982 and in 1983 based on building permits and starts of new buildings.

Other Factors

In the decade of the 80's new household formations are estimated at 13.6 million, but only 1.1 million will have two children or more. So, 92% of household formations will require two bedrooms or less — an obvious source of demand for apartments.

The Economic Recovery Tax Act of 1981 provides substantial advantages for the ownership of residential properties compared to commercial properties. Under ERTA, ordinary income recapture of accelerated depreciation declines in the ownership of residential housing and is fairly negligible after eight to ten years of ownership. In addition, maximum depreciation benefits are available for purchasing existing residential properties. New construction is no longer favored with special tax breaks.

Pension funds and other institutional investors still are actively pursuing real estate investments. Traditionally, buying has been concentrated in shopping centers and office buildings. In general, these types of properties appear in oversupply in many major markets. We anticipate some shift in institutional investment policy toward the purchase of residential properties.

Publicly Registered Partnerships

A strong case can be made for investing through the medium of larger publicly registered partnerships specializing in apartment acquisition. The main reason is the advisability of diversification in apartment investments. Apartments have different investment characteristics than shopping centers and office buildings. To make a long story short, it's much tougher to create a steadily rising cash flow in apartment projects because there are: 1) no cost passthroughs to tenants; 2) short leases making properties more subject to community and economic changes; 3) tenant turnovers requiring extensive maintenance and repair expenditures and intensive management and, 4) possibilities of rent control in some areas.

Unless you can diversify in private placements by planning a quarter of a million dollars or more of apartment investments, publicly registered partnerships are probably your best bet. In the first place, the major syndicators have pretty good batting averages, and in general, these public partnership investments have worked out well for investors. You can pick the partnership that has a sponsor whose acquisition philosophy you like. For instance, some sponsors buy apartments primarily for conversion to condominiums. Some purchase in the Sun Belt. Some specialize in lower-priced markets and properties.

The ownership of apartments is considered management intensive. With a diversified portfolio of properties, the general partner can balance the partnership's needs for current cash flow with the necessity to make property improvements to create better values in the longer term. Larger management companies may benefit from volume purchasing, for instance of carpets. Systems of financial controls and accounting are frequently superior in larger companies.

In the credit markets of today, financial clout and sophistication are important ingredients in the acquisition process. The large real estate syndicators develop a tremendous data base of property price information and are both good buyers and good sellers of property when the time comes.

Finally, the acquisition price of the property in a public partnership will be "at the market." The cost of the property to the syndicator will be the cost to the partnership (only increased by stated acquisition fees equivalent to a real estate commission). Typically, but not always, in private placements the purchase price of the property to the partnership is substantially higher than market. The syndicator adds to the cost by imposing financial instruments such as wrap-around mortgages. These types of transactions can result in substantial markups of property values. Inflated purchase prices are hard to overcome with appreciation if you are anticipating a short holding period of six or eight years.

BUY INCOME PROPERTIES NOW

Assuming a continuation of the current economic scenario, it's a fair bet that prices of existing real estate properties have nowhere to go but up. Price rises might even accelerate. First, we'll present our case for real estate and then tell you why you can profit personally by investing in publicly offered real estate limited partnerships.

Real estate prices are determined by the interaction of many variables. To name a few: urban/suburban, big/small, commercial/residential, financing, condition, location, credit of tenant, length of lease, market (competition), current return/upside, and price/replacement cost.

Overall pricing yardsticks have been pretty much tossed out the window today in favor of a much more detailed analysis of the various components of value. Value concepts such as rent multipliers, capitalization rates, costs per square foot and depreciated replacement cost are useful but cannot be relied on exclusively in judging relative prices. In other words, properties are not homogeneous. Each is a separate business with distinct characteristics.

In the long run, macroeconomic and demographic trends will affect real estate prices and values. Transportation costs favor close-in locations and multi-use types of properties. Energy costs are a factor in evaluating the type of construction and whether such costs can be passed through to tenants. Affordable housing means smaller unit sizes. The largest population growth segments are under 35 and over 60; so, there are implications for the warmer climates and urban areas.

Demand/Supply Factors

Both demand and supply factors will influence the course of real estate prices. Let's look at the demand side first. By world price standards, U.S. real estate is cheap, and our relative political stability and economic strength encourage foreign direct investment here. Rent levels, and hence prices, are lower by one-half in most cases in our cities compared with any major city in Western Europe. Foreigners are more comfortable with lower mortgage leverage than we are, so they can operate in our current mortgage market conditions.

Insurance companies and pension funds are no longer content with debt positions in real estate investments but now look for equity positions. Twenty-two percent of pension funds with over $500 million in assets held real estate investments in their portfolio at the end of 1980 versus 15% one year earlier (according to Greenwich Research Associates), an increase of 50% in one year. Pension funds are the fastest growing investment pool in the U.S., and most observers expect their trend toward real estate purchases to continue.

Rising replacement costs lift the umbrella for prices of existing property. As a rule of thumb, older properties (but not yet functionally or economically obsolete relative to newer properties) sell at a 20% to 25% discount from current replacement costs. Material prices in new construction and other construction costs (labor, for instance) have risen over 10% compounded per annum since 1973, faster than the Consumer Price Index. And, in this inflationary environment, the penalty in additional cost has been quite stiff for delaying a decision to build or buy.

High interest rates and recession traditionally take their toll on real estate development and are doing so again. The result will be a period of increased property sales which will tend to depress prices somewhat. So, it's a good climate to be buying properties.

A bear market is often described as a time when stocks return to their rightful owner. The same adage applies to real estate. The weak, nervous or financially troubled developer peels off some properties to generate cash and gain liquidity. The golden rule takes over — the guy with the gold rules!

The real estate business does have some problems today. Financial institutions are becoming developers through joint ventures and competing fiercely for the new supply of properties. Financing arrangements seem to be changing in character, either requiring more equity investment (less leverage) or variable interest rates. The current trend toward intermediate term, floating rate mortgage financing from banks is dangerous at best. So far, no mechanism exists to pass increased interest costs along to tenants. The typical fee structure in the real estate partnership business (mostly up-front at the time of purchase) can lead to insensitivity to acquisition price. Current returns (cash on cash) for properties are at new lows while other yields, or interest rates, are at new highs.

But, the severe difficulties the real estate business encountered in the middle seventies are nowhere in sight. Vacancy rates are low. Overbuilding is simply not a problem. Debt money is virtually unavailable which suppresses new construction activity. The business is pretty much in the hands of the "survivors" and the large players. No apparent financial problems or imbalances are brewing. The upward valuation of properties in the last several years is being matched by a torrid pace of increasing rent levels. We believe that a massive change in the country's basic economic fundamentals would be necessary to alter the continued favorable outlook for real estate prices.

In the next three chapters you will read about two popular real estate investments — net leases and subsidized housing. Both types of tax shelters can be good investments for the proper investor if they are priced fairly. Both are highly tempting because they provide the largest amount of tax loss of any real estate investment. We will discuss how to understand and evaluate net leases, and we will analyze current developments in subsidized housing.

NET LEASES

One of the most widely sold real estate tax shelters is the so-called net lease. These transactions have recently found their way to Wall Street. But, the newest game in town and the oldest profession in the world may have something in common — even after you've bought it, the person that sold it to you may still own it.

If the price and terms of long-term real estate net lease transactions aren't equitable you'll have no sensible economic choice but to give the property back when the tax lines cross. And, the guy that sold it to you or the tenant will end up owning it.

Real estate net lease transactions can provide tax losses, some regular cash flow and substantial residual value — all with a high degree of safety and predictability. The challenge is telling the difference between those that will live up to this promise and those that won't.

In a net lease transaction, you own a building occupied by a corporate tenant. The tenant agrees to pay rent and lease the property for an extended term. Also, the tenant pays any and all maintenance, repairs, insurance, taxes and operating costs — all the costs related to the occupancy and use of the property. You have no expenses except debt service — that's why it's called a net lease.

The primary term of the lease is for an extended period of time, say twenty-five years — a period sufficient for the rental income to completely amortize the cost of the property (recover the investment plus interest). At the end of the primary term of the lease, the tenant usually has the right to renew the lease for additional periods. These periods are of shorter duration, say five years, and are successive. The amount of rent for each period is stipulated in the lease and may be lower than the rent during the primary term.

External events are also covered in the lease. For instance, the property could be destroyed or condemned or no longer be economic for use by the tenant for a variety of reasons. If any of these developments occur, the tenant may make a lump sum settlement on a pre-arranged formula which is designed to recover your remaining investment. Normally, you have the right to reject this offer and cancel the lease. Obviously, you would do so if the property is worth more than the tenant is required to pay.

Frequently, the tenant has an option to repurchase the property and terminate the lease after the primary term. This offer is usually at fair market value but sometimes at a lower price (a so-called bargain repurchase offer).

So long as the tenant occupies the property, the property value will equal the income from the rent plus the residual value of the property when the lease expires. Based on present value today, the residual value when the lease expires isn't worth much. Example: How much would you pay today for a building you could sell for $10,000,000 twenty-five years from now? If you anticipated an 11% pre-tax return on your investment, you would pay only $687,665, or less than seven cents on the dollar. Looked at another way, $687,655 will equal $10,000,000 in 25 years at 11% interest compounded semi-annually.

High-grade corporate tenants usually don't have much trouble borrowing money — whether it's to finance their business inventory or their facilities. The corporation could use retained earnings, general corporate borrowings or a specific loan on the property (mortgage loan or net lease loan). So obviously, leasing a headquarters building is just an alternative to borrowing.

The corporation will look at occupancy cost, the rent it pays under the lease, and try to make the best deal. With a long term lease and a mortgage on the property as security, an institutional lender, such as an insurance company, will advance 100% of the property acquisition and development costs. So, the tenant's occupancy cost becomes the interest and principal payments on the loan (the debt constant).

If the corporation retains title to the building but borrows 100% of the purchase price, interest payments and depreciation are deductible occupancy costs. Principal repayments are not deductible. If the corporation gives you title to the property and pays you rent equal to interest and principal payments on the debt for 100% of property cost, all the rent is deductible by the corporation. And, you depreciate the property.

In the capital markets today, if a corporate tenant conveys the property to an institution, the annual rent to lease back the property will be about one quarter of one percent less than the interest rate would have been if the property cost had been borrowed. Multiply this rate by the property cost and you have the annual rent.

Traditionally, individuals have been willing to accept even lower rents than institutions because depreciation deductions have more value to them. Reason: The maximum tax bracket for individuals was 70% prior to January 1, 1982 but only 46% for a corporation. So, take less rent, but make it up in additional tax savings. That should be a fair trade off. No wonder net lease investments became so popular and still are, even though the top tax bracket for individuals has dropped to 50%. But, you want a good one, one that's priced fairly.

Most syndicated real estate net lease deals are fully leveraged — a lender advances 100% of the property acquisition and development cost. So, start out with the knowledge that not all of the amount you put up goes into the property — but rather to the tenant or the syndicator instead. Read the offering memorandum carefully to see how much of these payments goes to the sponsor of the transaction and how much to the tenant.

Most of the time, with good credit tenants (or lessees), a good portion of your cash investment goes to the tenant. It's a rental concession in one form or another. The rental concession may take the form of paying more for the property than the cost; allowing the tenant to occupy the property for no rent, or reduced rents, in early years; or paying debt service costs or other costs for the tenant. The rental concession today is the equivalent of about 150 basis points. The tenant's rent will be lower than his debt rate.

In many instances, rental concessions that are negotiated at arm's length don't favor the sponsor of the transaction and do reflect the true market. That's because many net lease transactions are put up for bid. But, obviously the sponsor selling you the net lease made the high bid, the one that gives the tenant the lowest occupancy cost. One way to be sure you're not doing business with a sponsor that chronically and substantially overpays (bids high) is to ask what the second highest bid for the property was.

If you don't get an answer, don't make the investment.

After you determine how much you're paying the tenant, then the rest of your cash investment goes to the sponsor-syndicator and the broker. Amounts paid to the sponsor above twenty percent of your cash investment are excessive. And, it doesn't matter what the payments are called — fees for services, profit on sale if the syndicator bought the property and resold it to the partnership, or syndication and organization fees.

A popular arrangement today is the syndicator's deferred fee. The amount starts out small but accrues interest so that over 15 or 20 years the obligation amounts to a large part of the residual value of the property. Watch out for this one!

Also, include in the syndicator's compensation the present value of the mortgage notes due him, if any, at the end of the primary lease term and the present value of land rent or the residual value of the land if the syndicator "carves it out" of the transaction. (The partnership frequently only buys the buildings and the syndicator takes the land for a small amount of cash. That's called carving out the land.)

You have to be very careful when you don't own the land. Even though you own the building, you become a tenant of the land owner, and the terms of your tenancy are embodied in a separate lease. Commonly, when this lease expires, you lose everything — your only option is to remove your building from his land which isn't very practical. So, the terms of this lease (which is usually called a ground lease) can make or break the transaction from a long-term point of view.

You'll be told there's a tax reason for the carve-out. The land is not depreciable, so carving out the land makes all of the purchase price paid for the property deductible. But, the land is irreplaceable. Unless the ground lease terms are so favorable that you don't suffer economically, you should always own the land. If you don't, you could be giving away all the residual value of the entire property for a very minor current tax advantage.

The quick way to see if you're paying a fair price is to compare your cash investment, plus interest on any delayed payments, to the underlying debt. This calculation is valid if none of the debt is held by the syndicator and if the underlying debt equals 100% of the property acquisition and development cost. If your investment is larger than about 30% of the amount of the debt, you're paying too much for the investment.

If the syndicator holds some debt, add the amount to your cash contribution and compare the total with the real underlying debt. Or, subtract the syndicator's debt from the total debt on the property. Again, if the cash investment is more than 20% to 30% of the debt, you are paying too much. (It's possible, but very unlikely, that this calculation could be misleading if you're acquiring older properties — but only if the underlying lease expires quickly or if the lease renewals are likely to be at higher rents than during the primary term of the lease.)

Economic Benefits

In a net lease investment, you think you're buying real estate but you're really not. Discounting the residual value to the present yields a tiny figure in relation to your current investment. You're buying tax deferral, usually for 10 or 12 years. Then there's a 10 or 15 year period when the property produces taxable income but no cash flow. That's the result of declining depreciation deductions and increasing, nondeductible mortgage principal payments.

Finally, when the original mortgage loan is paid off, almost all of the remaining rent will be cash flow to you — taxable in its entirety. This cash flow will continue as long as the tenant exercises his renewal options.

Eventually, the tenant won't renew the lease, and you'll be free to charge market rent for the property to a new tenant or sell the property to realize its residual value. Remember: You're talking about twenty-five years at a minimum. Probably, the property will be tied up much longer if renewal lease terms set rents at bargain rates. The tenant will be reluctant to give up a property he can occupy cheaply or sub-let at a profit.

Analyzing the economic benefits of net leases is a complicated task. For one thing, net leases are structured with such a variety of techniques that it isn't easy to determine whether you'll stay with the property or sell it when the tax loss benefits run out. For another, refinancing will depend on future interest rates (probably not property value) and the lease terms during the renewal periods. Finally, economic and functional obsolescence are hard to predict when looking out thirty years or more.

As you can see, a net lease transaction may have more of the characteristics of a loan than an equity purchase of real estate. (Many well-structured net lease deals can combine the attractiveness of both, however.) And, the economic benefit pattern resembles a subsidized housing transaction where tax losses (income deferral) are the prime consideration. Use the following steps to calculate the real rate of return on a net lease:

1. Discount your cash contributions to the partnership (whether they are called capital or interest) to present value at 6%.
2. Compound and accumulate each year's tax savings and cash flow at 6% per annum until the year the tax cost exceeds the cash flow (the cross-over point).
3. Discount at 6% all future cash flows after the cross-over point to present value at the date of cross-over. Consider this amount the hypothetical sale proceeds, and then subtract taxes due on the sale.
4. Find the interest rate that will compound the original investment to the total of the value of all economic benefits above. This calculation is more fully described in "The Best Way To Compare Tax Shelter Investments," p. 197.

The rate determined by this method is the real after-tax return on investment. Your target is 9% or better for the net lease investment to be fairly priced.

IMPACT OF THE NEW TAX LAW ON SUBSIDIZED HOUSING, NEW CONSTRUCTION AND REHABILITATION

The Good News: "ERTA" affects subsidized housing transactions favorably. The reason: Faster depreciation is allowed under the new Accelerated Cost Recovery System ("ACRS").

Rates of return will probably increase by 15% to 20% for new construction completed after January 1, 1981, assuming investor purchase prices don't change. And, investors who bought syndications in 1980, and in 1981 where properties are completed in 1981 or later, will have significantly increased tax deductions.

The Bad News: Returns will remain relatively low, less than 8% after tax per annum. The reason: Benefits of faster depreciation write-offs are partially offset by a reduction in maximum tax savings (tax rate) to 50% in 1982 and thereafter.

The Best News: Rehabilitation of certified historic structures into low-income housing projects will be the most attractive for all taxpayers. A sixty-month write-off of the rehabilitation expenditures has been replaced with a 25% investment tax credit. The investment credit could return most of an investor's cash purchase price. So, the prices paid to developers for these projects probably will increase.

A trend may develop for re-syndication, or the resale, of existing low-income projects. The reason: These old projects, if purchased after January 1, 1981, can be depreciated faster under the new rules by a new owner than by the original owner using the old, less favorable rules. With the reduction in individual tax rates, the original investors may not be getting the tax savings they bargained for. Also, the reduction in capital gains tax rates to a maximum of 20% makes selling for the original limited partner more profitable. (See the next chapter, "Sale of Older Subsidized Housing Partnerships Advisable.")

Subsidized housing (primarily the "Section 8" program) refers to a multi-family residential property for low and moderate income tenants where a portion of their rental payments are subsidized by the federal government. A below market rate mortgage is usually obtained from a federal or state agency. In return, rent increases are regulated by the government and cash distributions to investors are limited.

It's too early to tell whether prices of new construction Section 8's or rehabilitation transactions will increase. Because of the Reagan budget cuts, a decreasing number of projects will be subsidized. This reduction in supply and the increased tax benefits in early years will exert upward pressure on prices. On the other hand, reduced tax rates and increased tax benefits of non-subsidized real estate will mean fewer buyers for subsidized projects.

Investments in new construction subsidized housing probably aren't suitable for a married couple with projected 1984 taxable income of less than $60,000. The tax deductions (the major attraction of these transactions) would only be utilized in the 38% tax bracket during most of the tax period. Only taxpayers anticipating over $109,000 of taxable income in 1984 are suitable investors for these transactions.

Our conclusions for subsidized housing based on an analysis of the new tax law are:
- Prices for Section 8 new construction could rise by as much as 15% to 20%.
- Prices for certified historic rehabilitations will probably increase to keep returns in the same range as other subsidized transactions.
- The investment pay-in period for certified historic rehabilitations will be shortened to match the accelerated tax benefits.
- Most partnerships probably will not utilize the increase in the Section 167 (k) sixty-month amortization of rehabilitation expenditures from $20,000 to $40,000 per unit. The profit limitation upon sale is too stiff to justify the faster write-offs.

- Re-syndications of existing low-income projects may become popular to take advantage of the new depreciation rules.
- The large tax benefits received in subsidized housing enable you to own an attractively leveraged piece of real estate with little out-of-pocket cash. Even though it will be 20 years before you'll know the potential economic value because of governmental restrictions, these investments will remain popular.
- Investment decisions should continue to be based on traditional real estate selection criteria. Location, type of tenants, cost per unit or per square foot, type of construction and management are the most important factors in determining residual value.

Tax Changes

Shelter losses save less taxes under ERTA because the maximum tax rate has been reduced from 70% to 50%. But, taxes due upon the sale of tax shelters are less. The capital gains tax has been reduced from 28% to 20% and depreciation recapture is at a maximum rate of 50% vs. 70%.

With the reduction in maximum tax rates to 50%, earned and unearned income are taxed according to one rate schedule. Tax preference items (like the difference between accelerated and straight-line depreciation) no longer cause earned income normally taxed at a 50% rate to be taxed at higher rates. In the past, some deductions in subsidized housing transactions caused this shifting effect. Now, actual tax savings are easier to calculate because this shifting effect is eliminated.

New depreciation write-offs increase tax deductions in early years. In the first six years of ownership, you can now write off 54% of the cost of the building versus 38% under the old law.

The new depreciation methods are mandatory and are I.R.S. audit-proof. The reasonableness of depreciation assumptions in tax loss projections you'll find in offering memorandums is no longer a factor in your investment decision. Investments will now be easier to compare because depreciation will no longer be a variable.

Here's a comparison of the old and new depreciation schedules for new construction:

Depreciation Schedule

Year	Old Law 200% D.B.*	New Law 15-Year 200% D.B.
1	4.7%	7%
2	7.7	12
3	7.2	11
4	6.6	9
5	6.1	8
6	5.5	7
7-15	37.0	46
16-30	25.2	—
TOTAL	100%	100%

*Assumes a weighted average useful life of 30 years for a high-rise structure placed in service in July of the initial year of depreciation. D.B. = Declining Balance.

Impact On Tax Savings And Rates Of Return

Your tax savings in the first five years of a new construction investment are increasing 25% - 30% over the old law (assuming deals are priced the same). Write-offs for Section 167(k) projects, using $20,000 per unit amortization, do not change significantly. The table on the following page summarizes how tax savings stack up under the new law for different types of transactions.

Rates of return will probably increase for all types of subsidized housing. Under the old law, we calculated conservative adjusted rates of return for new construction, non-historic rehabilitations and certified historic rehabilitations to be in the 6% to 6.5% range. As shown in the table on page 144, the new returns will probably be in the 7% to 7.5% range, a 15% to 20% increase.

New Law Tax Savings — 50% Taxpayer
(000's)

Year	Investment	New Construction Section 8 (High-rise Building)	Rehab 167(k) $20,000*	Rehab 167(k) $40,000**	Certified Historic Rehab
1982	$ 8	$ 3	$ 3	$ 3	$ 3
1983	11	11	14	16	35 (1)
1984	10	12	13	16	6
1985	9	12	12	13	5
1986	7	9	8	12	5
1987	—	6	7	10	4
1988	—	4	6	5	4
1989-98	—	22	12	—	26
	$45	$79	$75	$75	$88

Tax Savings Under Old Law — 64% Bracket

	$45	$67	$67.7	N/A	$64.7

(1) Includes Investment tax credits of $28,000.

* Rehabilitation costs up to $20,000 per apartment unit amortized over 5 years. Remainder of expense depreciated over 15 years.

** Rehabilitation costs up to $40,000 per unit amortized over 5 years.

Note - This table does not include taxes that would be due upon foreclosure in 1998 of $23,000, $28,000, $28,000 and $25,000, respectively, for each investment shown above.

Subsidized Housing
Rates of Return

	Adjusted Rate of Return For 1984 Tax Bracket of*			Internal Rate of Return For 1984 Tax Bracket of**		
	42%	45%	50%	42%	45%	50%
Section 8 - New Construction	6.5%	6.9%	7.3%	9.7%	12.1%	14.6%
Section 167(k) Rehabilitation — Amortization of $20,000 per unit over 5 years	6.2	6.7	7.2	7.8	10.3	14.1
Section 167(k) Rehabilitation — Amortization of $40,000 per unit over 5 years	6.7	7.1	7.6	10.8	13.4	18.7
Certified Historic Rehabilitation	8.1	8.3	8.7	21.1	22.3	23.9

* Assumes constant after tax reinvestment of 6% over the life of the investment.
**Represents the rate of return on principal plus the rate of return of principal. The sinking fund method was used at 6% to pay the tax cost of foreclosure.

Note: Calculations are for a 1981 investment with the building placed in service in July 1982. Assumes all properties are foreclosed in seventeenth year of ownership. Rates of return are after tax per annum. Tax savings for a married individual were calculated using current tax rates phased into the indicated bracket in 1984.

Summary Of New Tax Law Provisions
Affecting Subsidized Housing

Property Type	Expenditure	Old Law	New Law
New Construction.*	All Construction Costs.	200% D.B. over assets' useful lives ranging from 5 to 45 years. Composite useful lives were from 23 to 33 years depending upon construction type.	200% D.B. over 15 years.
Rehabilitation of a nonhistoric property (I.R.C. 167 (K)).*	Purchase of existing building.	125% D.B. over useful life (normally 45 years).	200% D.B. over 15 years.
	Rehabilitation expenditures.	60-month write-off up to $20,000 per apartment unit.	Option to increase 60-month write-off up to $40,000 per unit.
	Treatment of excess over $20,000 or $40,000 limit.	Accelerated depreciation over useful life, normally 6 to 45 years.	200% D.B. over 15 years.
	Profit limitation on sale.	No legal restriction.	Essentially restricted to recovery of original investment if more than $20,000 per unit is written off over 60 months.
Rehabilitation of certified historic structures.**	Purchase of existing building.	125% D.B. over useful life (normally 45 years).	200% D.B. over 15 years.
	Rehabilitation expenditures.	60-month write-off (I.R.C. 191 - repealed effective 1/1/82).	15-year straight line depreciation. 25% investment credit of rehabilitation expenditures (I.R.C. 48 and 168).

* New law effective 1/1/81
** New law effective 1/1/82

Abbreviations:
D.B. - Declining Balance Depreciation
I.R.C. - Internal Revenue Code Section

SALE OF OLDER SUBSIDIZED HOUSING PARTNERSHIPS ADVISABLE

If you've owned a subsidized housing project for five years or more, you should investigate selling the entire partnership. The reasons: You've already received the majority of the tax benefits, and a new buyer should be willing to pay you as much or more than you paid for it. The real clincher is you probably can sell it for as much now as you could five years from now. So, why wait?

ERTA's the reason we offer this advice. Because of new depreciation rules, a new investor can depreciate a second-user property as fast as a new property and probably faster than you are depreciating it. That makes second-user subsidized housing properties worth more than before. Mathematically, they may be worth at least what you paid for them. Previously, second-user real estate was depreciated under much less favorable rules. So subsidized housing deals didn't have favorable resale value relative to cost in the early years of ownership.

Thanks to the new tax act, you may have liquidity in an investment that previously you thought you were locked into. And, the taxes you'll pay on the gain are much lower than before — a 50% maximum on depreciation recapture (versus up to 70% previously) and a maximum capital gains tax rate of 20% on the balance of the gain. Call up your general partner and find out how he plans to get you out.

A sale now will result in a higher rate of return than you should have ever thought possible. And, believe it or not, if you wait five more years to sell, you'll probably receive the same sales price. Why not get the cash in hand today? Unlike unsubsidized real estate, most properties will not increase in value until the government housing contract expires — probably not sooner than 10 to 15 years! In the meantime, benefits of ownership are limited to the tax savings. (If your property is well managed, cash distributions are possible but are restricted in amount by law.)

Will someone pay you your original purchase price for a subsidized housing deal? Yes, because the buyer's tax savings probably won't differ much from those offered by a new construction syndication, and rates of return will be just as attractive. The table below shows tax savings of $75 for the buyer of a re-syndication versus $79 for a new Section 8, hardly a substantial difference. And, the rates of return are almost identical.

Comparison Of Tax Savings
(000's)

Year	Investment	New Construction	Re-syndication
1982	$ 8	$ 6	$ 7
1983	15	14	12
1984	10	11	10
1985	7	9	9
1986	5	8	8
1987	—	6	6
1988	—	4	4
1989-96	—	21	19
TOTAL	$45	$79	$75
Adjusted Rate of Return*		7.3%	7.2%
Internal Rate of Return**		14.6%	14.6%

* Assumes reinvestment at 6%.
**The sinking fund method was used at 6% to pay the tax cost of foreclosure.

Note: Assumes 75% of the new investment is depreciable. 10% represents non-deductible syndication costs and 15% is organization costs that are deductible over 5 years. Rate of return calculations assume the properties are foreclosed in the seventeenth year of ownership.

Other attractions for the buyer are numerous. He won't have to worry about the substantial risks of construction and of rent-up (i.e., getting tenants). He'll benefit from a much lower mortgage rate than would be available currently and from knowing the property is viable in the market.

There are also further reasons to sell. Future tax losses are not substantial after the sixth year of ownership. If you've held the property for six years, you've already received 73% of your total tax savings. Future tax savings will be at a maximum rate of 50%, not the 65% or 70% rate you may have planned on.

Unfortunately, a tremendous conflict of interest may exist between you and the general partner. The general partner has already been paid a substantial portion of his fees in cash. But, his "residual value" fee (percentage of sale proceeds after you've received your investment back in cash) will not amount to anything if you sell now. He may want to wait another fifteen years and hope the project can be sold for considerably more than its tax loss value. But, you are better off if the project is sold now. Good luck.

Finally, it's far from clear how to sell these partnerships given the involvement of state and federal housing authorities in the projects. New and uncharted waters can be dangerous. Selling makes enough economic sense, though, to look into it carefully.

Let's assume you sell a five-year-old property for the same price you originally paid for it — $45,000. If selling costs of resyndication are 25%, you will receive cash of 75% of the selling price. Calculate taxes due at a 50% rate for 30% of the gain subject to recapture and at a 20% capital gains rate for the remainder of the gain. Your net proceeds of sale and the total economic benefits of ownership and sale are shown on the following page.

Sale Of Existing Property In 1982

Tax Savings thru 1981	$47,000
Less: Original Investment	− 45,000
Cash received on Sale	+ 33,750
Taxes due on Sale	− 20,000
Net Benefits of Ownership After Tax	$15,750

	Actual Return	Original Projected Return
Adjusted Rate of Return	9.5%	6.1%
Internal Rate of Return	13.5%	7.2%

OTHER SHELTER INVESTMENTS

VENTURE CAPITAL — R & D PARTNERSHIPS

Venture Capital or Research and Development partnerships are a newer type of tax shelter. In Research and Development ("R & D") partnerships, the limited partner investor puts up capital and the general partner transfers to the partnership know-how and patents (or merely a concept) on a product, process, formula or invention. The partnership makes the research and experimental expenditures to develop a prototype. Usually, this prototype is then licensed for manufacture by an affiliate of the general partner. As the end-product is successfully marketed, the R & D partnership earns royalties or license fees.

Several large private placements of R & D limited partnership interests have been completed. The two most well-known were for the DeLorean motor car and the Lear Fan business aircraft. Both were handled by Oppenheimer & Co. which raised about $48 million of limited partner equity in total for the two transactions. Also, in the last few years, many much smaller offerings have come out of the Silicon Valley region in California because high technology and electronics are well suited to this type of venture capital financing. The largest public offering has been Trilogy Ltd., a $60 million financing for a new computer.

Unfortunately, a number of promoters have entered the sweepstakes, so you must be wary of many of these transactions. The most outrageous example we have seen is the sale of a patent for $4.5 million to a newly formed limited partnership. Deep in the footnotes to the financial statements is the remarkable disclosure that the general partner bought the same patent 90 days earlier for only $20,000!

Another type of related offering is the license, franchise or distribution agreement shelter in which you buy rights or pay fees to market a product and make payment with cash and non-recourse notes. For tax purposes, you amortize the payment rapidly, or try to write it off immediately. Then you pay off the note from income earned selling the product. In general, these deals are economic rip-offs and probably won't generate promised tax deductions.

In an R & D partnership, you're really making a first-stage venture capital investment. There are two tough problems in analyzing an R & D partnership: understanding the business economics and determining whether the deal you're offered is fair. Obviously, each partnership will be involved in a new and completely separate venture so the business aspects require considerable study and knowledge.

There is a vibrant and growing venture capital market for this type of investment. Depending on numerous factors, providing this first-stage financing earns the capital partner a 40% to 60% interest in the business venture. Since the R & D partnership is in fact the capital partner, it too should receive a substantial stake in the enterprise to compensate for the risk involved. Taking all the capital risk for a relatively minor royalty interest, or a return that is limited to some modest payback formula, is unreasonable.

Using a partnership to finance such R & D expenditures has many advantages over a corporation, so you can expect to see more and more transactions of this type. Now let's discuss how R & D partnerships are put together and consider their tax and other advantages.

Tax Aspects

Under Section 174 of the Internal Revenue Code, a taxpayer may elect to deduct as an expense "research or experimental expenditures" when paid or incurred. The phrase "research or experimental expenditures" generally includes expenses for research and development in the experimental or laboratory sense, such as the costs to develop a prototype, plant process, product, formula or invention, or to improve similar existing properties. Deduction of these expenditures is only allowed in connection with a trade or business.

The R & D partnership seeks to qualify virtually all of its expenditures as deductible expenses of this type. Research and development takes time. Frequently, the limited partner feeds in his capital in installments over a period of two or three years. The result is nearly a 100% write-off for each installment.

Legal opinions for these transactions usually state that if the expenditures are of a research and experimental nature, they are deductible. But, no opinion is expressed as to whether the expenditures are research and experimental expenditures. Further, there may be a question of when the partnership's activities constitute a trade or business and hence when the expenditures are deductible.

R & D partnerships which are set up to receive royalties eventually seek to qualify such income as long-term capital gains. Here the partnership acquires technology and puts it to use more than twelve months prior to entering into a licensing agreement for its exploitation. The anticipated economic useful life of the technology transferred to the licensee is less than the term of the license and qualifies under Section 1221 (or Section 1235) of the Code as a capital asset. The attempt is to treat the licensing agreement as a sale or exchange of property so that royalty payments are taxed to the limited partner at low capital gains rates.

At best, the tax character of this income is not certain, and the IRS has several possible approaches. One would be to invoke the tax benefit rule which requires recapture of gain as ordinary income to the extent of previously expensed items. Another would be to assert the technology transferred under the license is held primarily for sale to customers and is not a capital asset. The result here would be to tax the royalties as ordinary income not capital gain.

Advantages

From the investor's viewpoint, using a partnership is distinctly better than using a corporation for financing first stage R & D expenditures. R & D deductions save taxes immediately for an individual at a rate as high as 50% in 1982 and thereafter versus eventual savings on a carryforward basis at a 46% rate for a corporation. If the enterprise fails, the investor has gotten the benefit of an immediate deduction. If a so-called 1244 stock corporation (the type you would establish for a venture capital deal) fails, the investor benefits from an ordinary loss deduction but only when the securities become worthless. That's undoubtedly several years down the road, and such losses are limited to $50,000 per investor ($100,000 on a joint return). There is no limit on deductions in a partnership.

In the partnership, an investor's cash return can be a royalty on gross sales rather than bottom line profitability. Cash flow will start more quickly and may be taxed as a long-term capital gain spread out over the years, as opposed to more-highly taxed dividends if the corporate form is chosen. Finally, there's no dilution of the partner's interest in the enterprise for subsequent financing requirements of the licensee or manufacturer.

The company with the technology (or the inventor) derives substantial benefit as well. For one thing, more control is retained over the enterprise because limited partners are not permitted to participate in the day-to-day management of the partnership. For another, the agreement can provide for the sale of the results of the research back to the inventor's corporation; so, he retains control of exploitation of the invention.

Also, the inventor will own 100% of the manufacturing corporation when seeking second-round financing. This can mean less dilution of his equity. Finally, the tax advantages reduce the investor's risk. So, the investor should accept less of the invention's income potential in return for making the investment.

R & D partnership financing can be attractive to both the company (or inventor) and the investor. But, you must not lose sight of the essential venture capital nature of the activity. Only if the invention is successfully exploited will the investment create any economic value. Your up-front investment is, after all, buying an expense which may or may not develop a valuable asset.

OIL INCOME FUNDS

One of the rapidly growing segments of the oil and gas limited partnership business is income programs. There are now 15 or so income funds, up from 3 in 1977. Income funds accounted for about 28% of the total oil and gas partnership capital raised in 1981. One program sponsor alone, Petro-Lewis, raised $500 million dollars in 1981, almost equal to the capital raised by all oil and gas funds in 1978.

An oil income fund is organized as a partnership and purchases existing producing properties. Oil and gas is sold, operating expenses are paid, and remaining revenues are distributed to the partners. A portion of the distribution is a return of capital and is not taxed because of the Tax Code provision for "cost depletion" (equivalent to depreciation for real property). The balance of distributions is taxable. Unlike drilling funds, income funds don't generate immediate tax deductions, although cost depletion is a tax benefit.

What's the excitement all about? — inflation, rapidly rising oil and gas prices and no drilling risk. For instance, it appears that quite a number of Petro-Lewis' partnerships formed in 1976 through 1979 are worth two and one-half to three times the original investment. This performance is probably accounted for by the rise in crude oil prices from $14 a barrel to $38 during this period. In other words, product price inflation exceeded the provision for inflation implicit in the sponsor's purchase formula. Should that continue to happen, investors will continue to fare well.

Sponsors inform us they now make an assumption of 8% to 10% for product price escalation when determining the purchase price they pay for reserves. Only if inflation exceeds this level of escalation will investors earn higher rates of return than 8% to 12% pre-tax (depending on which rate of return calculation you like, see below) by investing in oil income funds. The reverse is also true — lower inflation reduces your return. Obviously, if a sponsor charges lower fees than average or buys reserves at better prices than average, limited partner investment results will be improved.

Returns Available in Income Funds

Today, producing properties are purchased on a 15% to 20% discounted cash flow basis. Translated, that means for every dollar of property acquisition costs, a partnership will pick up about $1.97 of future net revenues. To see how this works, we set out a typical production pattern for oil and gas reserves (translated to dollars), then we discounted the cash flow to present value at 20%.

Oil and Gas Production

Year	Cash Flow From Production (1)	Cash Flow Discounted at 20%
1	$ 4,000	$ 3,470
2	3,000	2,150
3	2,400	1,422
4	2,000	979
5	1,600	647
6	1,200	401
7	1,200	334
8	1,000	229
9	800	151
10	800	124
11	2,000 (2)	270
TOTAL	$20,000	$10,177 (3)

Ratio of Cash Flow to Discounted Cash Flow - 1.97/1

(1) Net of operating costs, but pre-tax.
(2) Assumes balance of production is sold at end of 11th year.
(3) Purchase price necessary to achieve a 20% discounted cash flow assuming cash received semi-annually.

The income fund would pay $10,177 to purchase $20,000 of net future revenues. But, this result to the partnership was calculated before up-front costs and the slice to the general partner were figured in. The average level of up-front costs for income programs is about 12% and the typical general partner's revenue share is about 15%.

You can adjust for up-front costs by dividing the $10,177 purchase price of reserves by .88 which equals a $11,565 purchase price for the limited partner. The limited partner's income distribution will equal 85% of partnership revenues, or $17,000 ($20,000 x .85). Net of partnership costs and the general partner's promotion, the limited partner is purchasing $17,000 of cash flow for $11,565, or $1.47 of revenues over eleven years for each dollar of capital investment.

Remember, the revenues are a return of investment as well as a return on investment because the oil and gas reserves will be exhausted at some point. Thinking of the annual cash distributions of income funds as a "yield" on investment is not accurate because it constitutes a return of principal as well as earnings.

In calculating the pre-tax rate of return for this type of investment, there are several approaches. You will surely reinvest the cash distributions you receive. One way is to estimate various reinvestment rates and calculate total return. At a 10% reinvestment rate, the Adjusted Rate of Return is 10.1% pre-tax. At a 14% reinvestment rate, the Adjusted Rate of Return is 12.7% pre-tax.

Another method is the so-called Internal Rate of Return. The Internal Rate of Return is the rate that discounts the cash flows to the amount of the investment. In this case, it's 10.0% pre-tax for you. Higher rates of inflation in product prices could improve the rates of return and vice versa.

How to Evaluate Deal Structures

With oil and gas income funds proliferating, how do you distinguish between them? Use our method of Net Investment Ranking, and you'll be able to cut through the first confusing factor — the enormous variation in deal structures.

For instance, total front-end costs (including brokerage commissions, offering and organization expenses, management fees and general and administrative charges) vary from 3% of your capital contributions to 31.1%! Your share of the partnership's revenues varies from 90% to 75%. And in some deals the general partner puts in no capital and in others as much as 15% of property acquisition costs.

How does the variation affect the investor? — less than 12% from one to the other, according to our Net Investment Ranking method, nowhere near the difference you would think.

The "average" deal terms of the fourteen currently registered income funds work out as follows: Front-end costs — 14.1% from initial capital contribution and 3% more from operating revenues; general partner investment — 6.4% of property acquisition costs; Revenue Sharing — 84.5% to you and 15.5% to the general partner.

Here's how you can compare the costs of different program structures:

1. Percent In the Ground - The object is to figure out what percentage of initial limited partner capital contributions actually purchases reserves. The front-end costs payable from capital contributions are expressed as a percentage and are always enumerated in the prospectus. Subtract the percentage from 100% and the result is the Percent In The Ground. Sometimes some front-end costs are paid from subsequent revenues and not capital contributions. Ignore these amounts for purposes of this first calculation.

2. General Partner Cost Percentage - Often the general partner will bear a percentage of partnership capital. The percentage is separately stated in the prospectus. The percentage may be zero.

3. Property Purchase Percentage - Add #1 and #2 above. The result is the total amount available to acquire producing properties expressed as a percentage of original limited partner capital contribution.

4. Revenue Share - Most of the time the limited partner's revenue share is expressed as a single percentage figure (say 80% or 85%). That's straight forward. But, sometimes the percentage varies "before and after payout." After the limited partner receives his investment back in cash, the general partner's percentage of subsequent revenues increases, and the limited partner's percentage decreases. Since ultimate returns from income funds are unlikely to be much more than twice original partner capital contribution (payout), just average the limited partner percentage before

and after payout. A 90% before payout - 80% after payout deal is equivalent to an 85% revenue share.

5. Fees Payable From Revenues - If you're looking at a structure where some "front-end costs" are paid from production revenues, not capital contributions, you need to make an adjustment. The amount is usually expressed as a percentage of initial limited partner capital contributions. Divide the percentage by two and consider the result the percentage reduction in total revenues to your account.
6. Net Revenue Percentage - Substract the resulting percentage in #5 from the Revenue Share in #4. The result is the Net Revenue Percentage to the limited partner's interest.
7. Net Investment Ranking - Multiply the Property Purchase Percentage (#3) by the Net Revenue Percentage (#6). The result is the Net Investment Ranking. The higher the Net Investment Ranking, the more revenue-producing assets are working for you.

To make it easy for you, the Net Investment Ranking for some registered income funds is presented below. The four best rankings are ConVest, ENI, Damson Institutional and HCW. The four lowest rankings are IGE, NRM, Energy Methods and Damson. The spread in Net Investment Ranking is from 70.9 to 79.4, or only 12%, surprisingly small.

Sponsor	Net Investment Ranking
ConVest	79.4
Damson Inst'l	78.6
Damson	74.0
ENI	77.9
Energy Methods	73.7
ENEX	74.5
GeoVest	76.3
HCW	78.5
Henderson	75.3
IGE	70.9
N.R.M.	71.3
Petro-Lewis	75.8
Whiting	76.4

Management

The business of oil income funds is purchasing existing producing properties rather than the more risky business of exploration. Much less variation in performance should exist among income programs than among drilling funds. But, one sponsor certainly can do a better job than another in oil and gas reserve acquisition because the process takes tremendous judgment. At best, estimating future production from oil and gas properties is an educated guess. The quantity of reserves you are purchasing is anything but certain. Often, there are no rational explanations for specific properties actually performing either better or worse than your expectations.

Then, not all investment philosophies will produce the same result. For instance, do you acquire deep natural gas reserves now commanding $9 an Mcf? Or, do you acquire shallow natural gas reserves currently selling about $3 an Mcf in hopes they will be redesignated as tite gas which might double the price? Do you buy oil in the ground or natural gas?

Many feel the trick to achieving above-average investment returns in acquiring producing properties is correctly analyzing prospects for secondary recovery, infill drilling or creating production from currently non-producing sands. Here, obviously a combination of technology, geology and reserve engineering could pay significant dividends.

Most major oil and gas companies have property acquisition departments so the income fund business is competitive. Often, acquiring reserves can be cheaper on a cost per barrel basis than drilling for reserves. Many in the industry think finding costs for drilling and exploration were about $13 a barrel in 1981. On the other hand, producing reserves may be purchased today apparently at $10 to $12 a barrel.

Probably the biggest uncertainly relates to the future of hydrocarbon prices. Obviously, an optimistic scenario would justify a far higher purchase price than a conservative scenario. Sponsors typically figure some inflation in prices when determining bids for properties. So the actual course of future prices will have a large impact on how satisfactorily the investment works out.

ERTA IS NO BONANZA FOR EQUIPMENT LEASING

Contrary to popular opinion, ERTA does not provide a net favorable advantage for equipment lease investing for individuals. Reduced tax brackets restrict tax savings and the new method of depreciation, called the Accelerated Cost Recovery System ("ACRS"), only allows the 150% declining balance method for equipment placed in service through 1984 compared to the 200% declining balance method available under the old rules. The interaction of the new tax brackets and ACRS reduces the net present value of tax savings for investing in most equipment.

True, the new ACRS method allows capital recovery (depreciation) over a 5-year period, whereas under the old rules equipment normally leased by individuals was depreciable over a longer period of time (seven to ten years for drilling rigs and transportation equipment). The present value of depreciation is higher under ACRS.

But, if you were formerly in the 60% tax bracket or higher, the tax savings in your new 50% tax bracket are much lower than before. Even during the first three years, depreciation is only 10% or 15% higher now. Your reduction in tax bracket, 17% to 29%, exceeds the increase in depreciation, so your net tax savings benefit will be reduced.

There is plenty of good news in ERTA:

- There is no recapture of the 10% investment tax credit ("ITC") of the purchase price of equipment after 5 years of ownership versus 7 years previously;
- Because of the elimination of the 70% tax bracket, the major negative impact of tax preference items (the income shifting effect) will no longer harm equipment shelters for high-salaried investors;

- Recapture (taxation of depreciation in the event of sale) will generally be in the same tax brackets as the deduction;
- Gain on sale after depreciation recapture will be taxed at new lower capital gains rates;
- Since the depreciation period is shorter (5 years for most equipment), holding periods for investment may decrease, adding flexibility;
- ACRS is scheduled to change to the 175% declining balance method in 1985 and the 200% declining balance thereafter. When these changes are instituted, ACRS will deliver better net tax savings for investors than the old rules;
- ACRS is mandatory and audit proof (if you follow the rules, the IRS must accept the deduction), and uncertainty over the amount of first-year depreciation is no longer a factor.

Remember: Individuals are still subject to the rules requiring them to participate in operating versus finance leases to earn the ITC. Operating leases generally call for assuming risk in the investment. The initial lease period cannot exceed one-half of the ADR midpoint life (which is normally less than the estimated useful life rule under the old law), and you must pay operating expenses at least equal to 15% of lease income (among other requirements). All depreciation you take is still subject to recapture as ordinary income not as a capital gain, so you should always take the fastest cost recovery method available.

There are so-called "safe harbour" leasing transaction rules under ERTA applicable only to corporate lessors which are very attractive. Corporations can purchase "finance leases" on a highly leveraged basis and still earn the depreciation and the ITC. In reality, all other benefits of ownership including all of the residual value under these special provisions can accrue to the lessee. Corporations should be much more active than before in buying and selling equipment leases and will provide competition for individual investors for good leases. Our guess is that leases with a considerable measure of economic risk will be the ones offered to individuals.

The Calculations

The ACRS allows capital recovery through a percentage deduction of cost over the first five years of ownership (for most property) as follows:

ACRS
Personal Property

Year	Recovery Percentage*
1	15%
2	22%
3	21%
4	21%
5	21%
	100%

*For property placed in service in 1981-1984.

One method of comparing depreciation systems is to determine the present value of the deductions you are allowed. Under the new rules, generally all equipment is depreciable over five years (according to the table above.) Let's use an 8% discount rate to determine the present value of depreciation. Under the old rules, rail car depreciation was worth $37,683 (vs. a purchase price of $47,500). Using the same $47,500 unit of investment, depreciation on a drilling rig was worth $40,467. Under the new rules, the present value of the depreciation deduction is $40,603 for both types of equipment, no substantial advantage relative to the old rules. These calculations are contained in the table at the top of the next page.

Comparison Of Depreciation Methods

	Rail Car Old Rules		Drilling Rig Old Rules		All Equipment New Rules	
Year	Double Declining Balance	Present Value	Double Declining Balance	Present Value	ACRS Value	Present Value
1	$ 9,500	$ 9,500	$13,571	$13,571	$ 7,125	$ 7,125
2	7,600	7,037	9,694	8,976	10,450	9,676
3	6,280	5,384	4,847	4,156	9,975	8,552
4	5,024	3,988	4,847	3,848	9,975	7,918
5	3,819	2,807	4,847	3,563	9,975	7,332
6	3,057	2,080	4,847	3,299		
7	3,055	1,925	4,847	3,054		
8	3,055	1,783				
9	3,055	1,651				
10	3,055	1,528				
Total	$47,500	$37,683	$47,500	$40,467	$47,500	$40,603

But you must remember, depreciation is worth less to you because your tax bracket is lower. The offset — All personal property depreciation is recaptured on sale at up to the new maximum tax rate of 50%. So, now you'll pay a lower rate on recapture. The net present value of the tax savings less the present value of the recapture is the economic advantage of the tax deferral represented by an equipment lease investment.

The present value of tax savings is as much as 23% less under ACRS than under the old rules as shown below.

Present Value Of Tax Savings*

	Tax Bracket		
Old Rules	70%	60%	50%
Rail Car	$24,594	$21,717	$18,841
Drilling Rig	26,431	23,332	20,234
ACRS			
All Equipment	20,302	20,302	20,302

*Calculated by multiplying the present value of depreciation times the appropriate tax rate and includes the shifting effect of tax preferences under the Old Rules.

The present value of tax savings less recapture under ACRS is one-half to one-third of the old rules. In other words, the net tax benefit of equipment leasing (not considering the economic value) is lower under ERTA than before.

Present Value Of Tax Savings Less Recapture*

	Tax Bracket		
Old Rules	70%	60%	50%
Rail Car	$ 7,961	$ 7,460	$ 6,960
Drilling Rig	5,478	5,372	5,267
ACRS			
All Equipment	2,845	2,845	2,845

*8% discount to present value of tax savings and of cost of recapture (calculated assuming equipment was sold for original cost at end of the depreciation period). Assumes 50% tax bracket for ACRS calculation.

THOROUGHBRED HORSES

There are two basic segments of the Thoroughbred horse business: breeding and racing. The breeder mates the best horses and hopes to sell the offspring to those who want to put them into racing competition. In horse racing you hope to win money (purses) at the racetrack and put your best racehorses back into production (breeding) to start the cycle all over again. People breed horses to race, and racing is the testing market for breeding theories. Of course, it's more glamorous, and riskier, than this simple scenario, but that's basically what the Thoroughbred business is all about.

For 300 years, this industry has been tightly controlled by a relative handful of people. In the past several years, however, thousands of newcomers have poured into the market, some seeking excitement and social acceptability but most looking for tax benefits and financial reward — and a hedge against inflation. Prices of the best-bred horses at auction have dramatically outstripped the rate of inflation for the past decade.

For all their mutual dependency, breeding and racing offer quite separate attractions from an investment angle and some differences from a tax point of view. Each can be potentially lucrative, or disastrous, but the rules which govern racing have tended to tilt the investment scale toward breeding, especially in the past five years. Here are the main reasons.

In most of the 31 states where racing horses is legal, generally no more than 10 people can own a racehorse. In New York up to 15 can and in California, practically anything goes. The reason is so that people of known unethical behavior will not be associated with a sport whose lifeblood is gambling. By law, racehorse owners must be licensed (fingerprinted, etc.) and Thoroughbred racing is probably the best-policed sport in the world. Obviously, the ownership rule severely limits the number of people who can participate in buying racehorses.

Owning racehorses for winnings at the track seems like a tough business. Racehorses cost between $10,000 and $18,000 per year to keep in training on the racetrack, and mortality insurance carries a premium of 7% of the appraised value of the animal. So, a $100,000 racehorse costs about $25,000 per year to maintain. The average horse earns purses of less than $8,000 per year. (This figure may be misleading since it represents over 70,000 horses, most of which run at small tracks which offer small purses.)

But, horse racing can be profitable. At the country's major tracks, the majority of horses probably earn enough to pay their maintenance. At most tracks, nine races are run, six or seven days a week, and various tracks in racing states are open year-round (even in the North). Of the $8 billion legally bet last year on the races, almost half a billion went into purses. So, there's plenty of money to shoot at if you have a good enough horse.

Even if a racehorse is very good, the big money is in the breeding. Genetics in Thoroughbreds is of paramount importance, but performance on the track counts almost as much. The best racehorses produce the best racehorses. Here are costs and values of ten horses which were purchased as yearlings and subsequently raced well enough to be syndicated for breeding:

Horse's Name	Original Cost	Syndication* Value
Storm Bird	$1,000,000	$30,000,000
Spectacular Bid	37,500	22,000,000
Alleged	30,000	13,000,000
Seattle Slew	17,500	12,000,000
Noble Nashua	49,000	11,000,000
Lord Avie	11,000	10,000,000
The Minstrel	200,000	9,000,000
Timely Writer	4,500	6,000,000
Proctor	45,000	2,000,000

*Total price paid for the horse when it was sold for breeding.

Here are some examples of horses which were not syndicated for high prices but whose offspring have been so successful that the value of breeding shares in them has skyrocketed in a short period of time:

Horse's Name	Original Price Per Share*	Year Syndicated	Current Price Per Share
Blushing Groom	$160,000	1977	$300,000
Exclusive Native	60,000	1972	300,000
Icecapade	30,000	1973	150,000
Key to the Mint	150,000	1973	500,000
King Pellinore	40,000	1976	120,000
Lyphard	165,000	1977	650,000
Mr. Prospector	50,000	1975	600,000
Raja Baba	10,000	1972	125,000

*A "share" is the value of each unit purchased when the horse was syndicated (syndication value divided by the number of purchasers).

Experts feel there may have been a concentration of investor speculation in the breeding business. Now, there appears to be an oversupply of high-priced stallions on the market.

Thus, the breeding action may have begun to swing toward the acquisition of top-flight, or very well-bred, females (fillies on the track, mares when they are bred). A mare can produce only one foal a year, while a stallion can sire up to 40 or 50. But mares cost a lot less than stallions, and mares can be expected to produce six foals over their breeding careers. Each foal of a well-bred mare might sell for $65,000 or more. A mare can become a hot commodity (by her extended "family" doing well on the racetrack). Her value and the price her offspring bring at auction could rise dramatically. It's not uncommon for broodmares to return many times their cost over a period of time. Of course, most do not — but that's the challenge.

Like any speculative venture, Thoroughbred racing, or breeding, does involve inherent risks. These risks are somewhat mitigated by the tax advantages.

Horses and Taxes

Under ERTA, the depreciation schedules for horses have been simplified. The old hodge-podge of "useful lives" ranging up to 10 years has given way to the more liberal Accelerated Cost Recovery System ("ACRS") of depreciation over three, or five, years. Applicable depreciation rates boil down to a question of age and use of the horse.

In both racing and breeding, the pace of depreciation depends on the age of the animal at the time of acquisition. Racehorses "over the age of two," and breeding horses "over the age of 12," are depreciable in three years:

Depreciation Year	Percentage*
1st	25%
2nd	38%
3rd	37%

*For horses purchased from 1982 through 1984. In 1985 and thereafter faster depreciation is allowed.

Racehorses under the age of three and breeding horses under the age of thirteen are depreciable as follows:

Depreciation Year	Percentage*
1	15%
2	22%
3	21%
4	21%
5	21%

*For horses purchased from 1982 through 1984. In 1985 and thereafter faster depreciation is allowed.

It appears under ERTA you can still continue to depreciate over a three-year period a racehorse you purchase over the age of two even if you eventually send it off to the breeding shed.

There are two potential depreciation traps an unsophisticated investor can fall into as a result of ERTA. First, the definition of age has not been clarified by the IRS. The date a horse turns three or thirteen is not clearly defined. Here are the possible interpretations.

- Option One - A horse born on April 1, 1980, was officially one year old January 1, 1981 (the "universal" birthday).

To qualify for the fastest depreciation, a horse must be over the age of two (or twelve). Based on the universal birthday, the horse does not turn three until January 1, 1983. This concept of age is the most conservative;

- Option Two - By going with the actual foaling (birth) date of the horse, some advisors claim that a horse is "over" the age limit for depreciation twenty-four months and one day after it is foaled. According to this interpretation, a horse born April 1, 1980 would be "over the age of two" on April 2, 1982;
- Option Three - The most aggressive tax posture considers a horse "over" the maximum age limit on January 2nd of the year in which it officially (back to the universal birthday) becomes two or twelve years old, or January 2, 1982 in our example. Horsemen are lobbying for this interpretation with the IRS.

The second trap concerns the date on which either the investor enters the horse business or a limited partnership or other syndicate is organized. You can only take full depreciation if you're in the horse business in January of the calendar year (assuming the calendar year is also your fiscal year for tax purposes). Some partnerships are set up in January but do not buy horses or engage in any activity until December, the traditional peak of the sales season. Taking a full year's depreciation is questionable under these circumstances. A partnership organized in January at the very least should begin some operations right away even if modestly, in order to hope to take a full year's depreciation on horses bought in November or December.

IMPORTANT: Investors who breed horses to race rather than to sell cannot depreciate the offspring. And, capital gains treatment on sale may not be available for either the offspring or the breeding stock. That's because income could be subject to ordinary tax rates (sheltered by depreciation on the breeding stock and maintenance costs) if the taxpayer is recognized as a commercial breeder. This trap may be avoided by combining racing and breeding activities, but expert tax advice is required to draw these distinctions properly.

THE ECONOMIC RECOVERY TAX ACT OF 1981

ERTA AFFECTS TAX SHELTERS FAVORABLY

Tax Brackets and Rates

ERTA provided a dramatic reduction in tax rates for you. Rates will drop 23% through 1984 from 1981 levels. For 1981 you also got a 1.25% tax credit. The reduction is 10% each in 1982 and 1983 and 5% in 1984. The accompanying tables show how this across-the-board tax relief works.

The most dramatic early reduction in rates applied to the 70% income bracket which was reduced to 50% starting in 1982. With $215,400 of taxable income on a joint return, taxes drop to $95,149 in 1982, almost $22,000 lower than 1981 payments. Since the highest marginal tax rate on any income is 50% in 1982, the maximum tax limitation on personal service income has been repealed. Similarly, the tax on undistributed personal holding company income has been cut to a maximum of 50%.

Tax Rate Schedules - Married
(Joint Returns)

Taxable Income	1981* Tax Due + % on Excess**	1982 Tax Due + % on Excess**	1983 Tax Due + % on Excess**	1984 Tax Due + % on Excess**
$ 29,900- 35,200	$ 6,201 37%	$ 5,574 33%	$ 5,034 30%	$ 4,790 28%
35,200- 45,800	8,162 43	7,323 39	6,624 35	6,274 33
45,800- 60,000	12,720 49	11,457 44	10,334 40	9,772 38
60,000- 85,600	19,678 54	17,705 49	16,014 44	15,168 42
85,600-109,400	33,502 59	30,249 50	27,278 48	25,920 45
109,400-162,400	47,544 64	42,149 50	38,702 50	36,630 49
162,400-215,400	81,464 68	68,649 50	65,202 50	62,600 50
Over 215,400	117,504 70	95,149 50	91,702 50	89,100 50

* The rate schedule shown above for 1981 is the same rate schedule that applied for 1980 taxes. A taxpayer may use this schedule to find the approximate taxes due for 1981 by computing the tax under the schedule and reducing the results by the 1.25% tax credit.

** The tax rate on the amount by which the taxpayer's taxable income exceeds the base of the bracket.

Tax Rate Schedules - Single Individual

Taxable Income	1981* Tax Due + % on Excess**	1982 Tax Due + % on Excess**	1983 Tax Due + % on Excess**	1984 Tax Due + % on Excess**
$18,200- 23,500	$ 3,565 34%	$ 3,194 31%	$ 2,865 28%	$ 2,737 26%
23,500- 28,800	5,367 39	4,837 35	4,349 32	4,115 30
28,800- 34,100	7,434 44	6,692 40	6,045 36	5,705 34
34,100- 41,500	9,766 49	8,812 44	7,953 40	7,507 38
41,500- 55,300	13,392 55	12,068 50	10,913 45	10,319 42
55,300- 81,800	20,982 63	18,968 50	17,123 50	16,115 48
81,800-108,300	37,677 68	32,218 50	30,373 50	28,835 50
Over 108,300	55,697 70	45,468 50	43,623 50	42,085 50

* The rate schedule shown above for 1981 is the same rate schedule that applied for 1980 taxes. A taxpayer may use this schedule to find the approximate taxes due for 1981 by computing the tax under the schedule and reducing the results by the 1.25% tax credit.

**The tax rate on the amount by which the taxpayer's taxable income exceeds the base of the bracket. *as percentage of income*

The long-term capital gains tax has been reduced to a 20% maximum for all transactions after June 9, 1981. A one year holding period is still required for long-term rates to apply.

ERTA also reduced the top alternative minimum tax (AMT) rate from 25% to 20%. The tax is 10% for AMT income between $20,000 and $60,000 and 20% for any amount in excess of $60,000.

In 1985 and thereafter, taxes will be revised, or indexed for inflation to prevent "bracket creep." That means tax rate schedules and the $1,000 personal exemption will be adjusted annually to reflect the percentage by which the Consumer Price Index increases.

Depreciation and Investment Tax Credits

ERTA began a new system of recovery of capital costs for tangible depreciable property placed in service after 1980. All real and personal property is put into a 3-, 5-, 10- or 15-year class (statutory recovery period) for depreciation. Recovery percentages are applied to the entire purchase price (salvage value is disregarded). This system is called the Accelerated Cost Recovery System ("ACRS").

Personal Property

For personal property, the 150% declining balance depreciation method is available through 1984 (175% in 1985 and

200% thereafter). That means the write-off in the first year can be 150% larger (175% larger in 1985 and 200% larger thereafter) than the write-off allowed under straight line depreciation. You may also use a straight-line method over the recovery period (or certain specified longer periods). Both new and used property are allowed the same methods and periods. (Different rules apply to property used outside the United States.) The table below shows the annual recovery percentages for the various classes of personal property:

Recovery Percentage For Personal Property Placed in Service 1981-1984

If the recovery year is:	3-year	5-year	10-year	15-year public utility
1	25%	15%	8%	5%
2	38	22	14	10
3	37	21*	12	9
4		21	10	8
5		21	10	7
6			10	7
7			9*	6*
8			9	6
9			9	6
10			9	6
11				6
12				6
13				6
14				6
15				6

*Conversion to straight-line

The classes in the table above include the following kinds of personal property:
- 3-year - automobiles, property used in connection with research and experimentation, race horses;
- 5-year - most other equipment, except long-lived public utility equipment;

- 10-year - certain public utility property, railroad tank cars, residential manufactured homes, qualified coal-utilization property;
- 15-year - certain public utility property.

Gain on the sale or disposition of personal property is taxed as ordinary income to the extent of any ACRS deductions taken. As under the previous rules, the excess of ACRS deductions over the amount allowed had the straight-line method been used is an item of tax preference. For this calculation straight-line depreciation is computed over 5, 8, 15 or 22 years, depending on the respective property class.

Generally, no ACRS deduction is allowed in the year of disposition. Also a taxpayer cannot switch to the ACRS method for property acquired or used during 1980. And, the additional first year, or bonus, depreciation deduction has been repealed for 1981.

Furthermore, there are so-called anti-churning rules designed to prevent swaps of equipment between parties for the purpose of obtaining the new benefits of ACRS. In transactions not recording gain or loss, acquisitions from related persons and sale/leaseback transactions, the transferee must use the transferor's method in computing the ACRS deduction.

Real Property

The real property recovery period is 15 years, and ACRS percentages are based on the 175% declining balance method (200% for low-income housing). The IRS has supplied a table for the annual allowances over the recovery period. The first year recovery percentage allowable is determined by the number of months the real estate is in service in that year. If property is sold before the end of the recovery period, the ACRS percentage for the year of disposition will be based on the number of months during that year the property was in service. For all real property you can elect an optional recovery period using straight-line depreciation of 15, 35 or 45 years. Under ACRS, component depreciation is eliminated and composite depreciation is required for the entire building and components.

ACRS Tables For Real Estate
(Except Low-Income Housing)

The Applicable Percentage* is:
(Use the Column for the Month in the
First Year the Property is Placed in Service)

If the Recovery Year is:	1	2	3	4	5	6	7	8	9	10	11	12
1	12	11	10	9	8	7	6	5	4	3	2	1
2	10	10	11	11	11	11	11	11	11	11	11	12
3	9	9	9	9	10	10	10	10	10	10	10	10
4	8	8	8	8	8	8	9	9	9	9	9	9
5	7	7	7	7	7	7	8	8	8	8	8	8
6	6	6	6	6	7	7	7	7	7	7	7	7
7	6	6	6	6	6	6	5	6	6	6	6	6
8	6	6	6	6	6	6	5	6	6	6	6	6
9	6	6	6	6	5	6	5	5	5	6	6	6
10	5	6	5	6	5	5	5	5	5	5	6	5
11	5	5	5	5	5	5	5	5	5	5	5	5
12	5	5	5	5	5	5	5	5	5	5	5	5
13	5	5	5	5	5	5	5	5	5	5	5	5
14	5	5	5	5	5	5	5	5	5	5	5	5
15	5	5	5	5	5	5	5	5	5	5	5	5
16	—	—	1	1	2	2	3	3	4	4	4	5

*The applicable percentage is 6.67% in each year if the straight line 15-year alternative is selected.

Note: This table does not apply for short taxable years of less than 12 months.

The rules for taxing gain on property sales are also changed. For commercial property, all depreciation is taxed as ordinary income to the extent of the gain on disposition, if accelerated 15-year deductions are taken. Gain on fifteen-year commercial property for which the straight-line method is elected is taxed as a capital gain on sale. For all other real property, accelerated depreciation recapture (or recapture phase-out) remains the same as before.

As under the old law, the excess of ACRS deductions for real property over the amount allowed had the straight-line method been used is an item of tax preference. Bear in mind that the shifting effect, generally the most costly consequence of tax preference items, is eliminated in 1982 and thereafter because of the reduction in the maximum tax rate to 50%. That is, a tax preference item will no longer cause income normally taxed at a 50% rate to be taxed at 70%.

Investment Tax Credits

For 3-year eligible property placed in service after 1980, the investment tax credit ("ITC") is 6%. For 5-, 10-, 12- and 15-year eligible property the credit is 10%. In addition, ITC's have been increased for rehabilitating qualified buildings and historic structures. And, the rules governing credits for energy property and research and development expenditures have changed. (These new rules are discussed below.)

For property placed in service after February 18, 1981 (unless acquired pursuant to a binding contract entered into before February 19, 1981), the ITC is not allowed on investments that are not "at risk." This rule applies to individuals, Subchapter S Corporations and certain closely held corporations. Amounts are not "at risk" if (1) the taxpayer is protected against the loss, (2) the amount is borrowed and the taxpayer is not personally liable for the repayment of the debt, (3) the lender has an interest other than as a creditor, or (4) the lender is a related party to the borrower.

There is, however, an important exception. Non-recourse debt can, under some circumstances, increase the "at-risk" amount for ITC purposes. Here's how: You must at all times have a minimum "at-risk" investment of 20% of the property's basis; acquire the asset from an unrelated person; and owe the borrowed amount to an "unrelated creditor" (defined as a bank, insurance company, savings and loan, etc.). Also, an "unrelated creditor" may not own more than a 10% equity interest in the borrower, seller or promoter.

Sale or disposition of property during the new ACRS recovery period causes recapture of a portion of the ITC. For three-year property, the recapture percentage is 33% for sale in the third year, 66% in the second year, and 100% in the first year. For 5-, 10-, 12- and 15-year property, the recapture percentage for sale in the fifth through the first years of ownership are 20%, 40%, 60%, 80%, and 100% respectively.

Underpayment Penalties

ERTA contains a number of provisions applicable to 1981 tax returns that will take most of the fun and profit out of tax shelters bought for the sole purpose of delaying payment of tax. For one thing, the interest charge you pay on delinquent taxes is now 100% of the prime rate on October 15th of each year. Prior to ERTA, the rate was 90% of the prime adjusted every two years (the last two years a bargain rate of 12%.) For 1982 the rate is set at 20%. No more "bargains" from Uncle Sam.

Furthermore, if the reason for underpayment of taxes is a "valuation overstatement" (you claim more depreciation, ITC, etc. than you should), you are subject to a non-deductible penalty of as much as 30% of the tax underpayment. The penalty applies for overvaluations above 150% of real value and applies to any property acquired by the taxpayer within the five years preceding the close of the tax year for which the overstatement was made.

The stock in trade of most shoddy shelters is an overvaluation of property for depreciation or ITC purposes. Now, claiming a valuation higher than the realistic valuation can be painful because of a new overvaluation penalty. The new cost of these changes is outlined in "3 to 1 Write-Offs - Don't Try 'Em," page 191.

Real Estate and ERTA

The new ACRS depreciation rules are favorable for the purchase and the ownership of real estate. For new property, the 15-year depreciable life (ACRS recovery period) is generally considerably shorter than the weighted-average useful life reasonably employed under the old law. ERTA now allows more advantageous accelerated depreciation methods for the acquisition of used property as well, substantially larger than the allowable depreciation deductions under the old law. Furthermore, the new law eliminates arguments with the IRS about the amount of allowable depreciation because the approved methods are mandatory and audit proof.

The substantial increase in depreciation deductions for older properties should stimulate syndication, or re-syndication, of existing properties and also increase benefits for "existing property" syndications. The full impact is spelled out in Section Four, "Real Estate Tax Shelters".

Unlike the prior law, the ACRS rules allow residential and commercial property the same accelerated method of depreciation (175% declining balance). The excess of ACRS deductions over the allowable depreciation if the straight-line method had been used is an item of tax preference for both types of property. The significant distinction is that gain on disposition of commercial property is ordinary income to the extent of 100% of ACRS deductions. Whereas, for residential property, non-tax preference depreciation is recaptured as a capital gain.

The special status of low-income housing is preserved by the new law. Such housing is accorded a faster depreciation method (200% declining balance). Also, ACRS preference item recapture is phased out as under the past law. In addition, low-income housing is now permanently exempt from the requirement to capitalize and amortize construction period interest and taxes. You may write-off $40,000 per unit over 60-months for expenditures to rehabilitate low-income housing (Section 167-K). The former limitation was $20,000. The new limitation applies for expenditures made in 1981 and thereafter.

A new investment tax credit is available for rehabilitating qualified buildings and certified historic structures. The credit applies to expenditures incurred in 1982 and thereafter. The credit is 15% of rehabilitation expenditures for buildings 30-39 years old, 20% for buildings at least 40 years old and 25% for certified historic structures. Expenditures must be capitalized and depreciated on a straight-line method over a 15-year period, and there must be a substantial rehabilitation of the building. Only commercial properties can qualify for the 15% or 20% credit. The 25% credit is available for both residential and non-residential users. For rehabilitations other than certified historic structures, the cost of the property eligible for depreciation must be reduced by the credit allowed.

All rehabilitation construction plans of certified historic structures must be approved by the Secretary of the Interior as consistent with the historic character of the property. Structures in a "registered historic district" must be certified as nonhistoric before expenditures are eligible for the 15% or 20% credit.

The 60-month amortization of rehabilitation costs for non-subsidized housing historic structures is repealed. The 10% ITC for rehabilitating 20-year-old non-residential buildings is also repealed. There are special transition rules for projects under construction.

Oil & Gas and ERTA

The Windfall Profit Tax on newly discovered oil will be reduced in stages from 30% to 15% by 1986. The phase-down of the depletion allowance was not changed in the new law. Oil produced from so-called stripper well properties (generally producing less than ten barrels per day) is now totally exempt from the Windfall Profit Tax after 1982, if the following conditions are met: the oil must be produced by an independent producer; the oil must be attributable to a working interest in the property; and the property must have been acquired prior to July 23, 1981.

Qualified holders of royalty interests in crude oil production were entitled to a $1,000 credit against Windfall Profit Tax liability in 1980. For 1981, the credit was increased to $2,500. In 1982 and thereafter, the credit is replaced by an exemption equal to 2 bbls. of crude oil per day through 1984 and 3 bbls. per day thereafter (roughly $30,000 of annual income at today's prices). Neither the credit nor the exemption is available for production from overriding royalty interests, net profits interests, production payments or similar carved-out interests in properties acquired after June 9, 1981.

Equipment Leasing and ERTA

ERTA created a so-called safe harbour lease election for corporations. It did so by guaranteeing that a three-party finance and lease transaction is categorized as a lease for investment tax credit, cost recovery and other income tax purposes. Under ERTA requirements, all parties to the lease must categorize the lessor as the owner of the property. In addition, the lessor must have a minimum "at-risk" investment of not less than 10% of the adjusted basis of the leased property (maintained at all times during the lease); the lease cannot exceed the greater of 90% of the useful life of the property (Code Section 167) or 150% of the ADR class life; and the property leased must be "qualified leased property." These rules do not apply to non-corporate or individual lessors.

The main benefit ERTA offers individuals engaged in equipment leasing is the generally faster depreciation, or the generally larger depreciation deductions in early years, available under the ACRS system. This allows for faster recovery of capital costs. Also, when the tax lines cross and the property begins producing taxable income, the added income will be taxed no higher than 50%.

The "at-risk" limitation described earlier in the discussion on Investment Tax Credits must be considered. However, in general, the rules allow a tax credit for the amount of non-recourse debt from "unrelated" lenders as well as your cash or other "at-risk" investment. The ITC recapture rules still apply on disposition of property.

The new investment credit "at-risk" rules do not apply to amounts borrowed for qualified energy property. This exception is granted if the amount "at-risk" is at least 25% of the unadjusted basis for the property. Any non-recourse financing must be in the form of a level payment loan.

Commodity Straddles and ERTA

Significant rule changes have been enacted to curtail the use and effectiveness of commodities, futures and options, and tax straddles as shelters. The new rules are effective for property acquired and positions established after June 23, 1981.

Under ERTA, gain or loss for tax purposes on "regulated futures contracts" is determined by the contracts' fair market value on the last day of the year. Any unrealized capital gain or loss is treated as if realized — 40% is short-term and 60% is long-term. So, at the new maximum 50% tax rate, the maximum tax on the entire gain is 32% (40% @ 50% and 60% x 40% @ 50%). A transition rule allows you to pay in installments any taxes due on 6/23/81 positions. Otherwise, the new rules apply.

If a position or a straddle does not qualify as a regulated futures contract (for instance, a futures forward contract or option), a loss may be taken for a taxable year only in excess of unrealized gains on positions which were: acquired before the disposition giving rise to such loss; offsetting positions to the loss position; and not part of an "identified straddle."

There are two exceptions to these rules. You may elect to exclude a regulated futures contract from these provisions if only one of two positions is a regulated futures contract and you identify all of the straddle positions as part of a straddle. Losses on such "identified straddles" are deferred until the year the offsetting position is closed. The other exception is for a bona fide "hedging transaction" identified as such on the day the contract is acquired. Here, gain or loss is taxed as ordinary gain or loss. The exemption for a hedging transaction does not apply to transactions entered into by, or for, a "syndicate" (a partnership, or other entity, in which more than 35% of the loss is allocable to limited partners).

Current deductions of interest and carrying charges (cost to insure, store, or transport) may only offset current income generated from the position. The balance of such charges must be capitalized (except for hedging transactions). Also, cancellations of forward contracts for currency or securities now result in capital gain or capital loss, not ordinary income or loss.

Finally, the Secretary of the Treasury will develop new regulations for straddles that are similar to the wash sales and short sales rules applicable in other investment markets.

Securities Dealers and ERTA

The new commodity straddle rules just outlined diminish the attractiveness of "securities dealers" tax shelters as well. In addition, ERTA re-defines governmental obligations as capital assets if issued at a discount and payable without interest in less than one year. Any gain realized on sale or exchange is treated as ordinary income (interest) up to what is called the "ratable share of the acquisition discount." Gains in excess of this amount are short-term capital gains. The ratable share is the portion equal to the number of days the bill or note is held divided by the number of days between the date of acquisition and the date of maturity. This results in all gains being treated as interest income if there's no fluctuation in rates during your ownership of the obligation. Changes in rates will create gains or losses, a portion of which will be short-term capital gain or loss.

Dealers in securities are now required to report that a security is being held for investment no later than the close of business on the day the security is acquired (vs. 30 days later under the former rules). The inability to deduct excess interest and carrying charges also harms the securities dealer tax shelter.

R & D Shelters and ERTA

You can earn a new, non-refundable 25% tax credit for incremental research and experimentation expenditures made after June 30, 1981, and before 1986. The credit applies to 25% of the excess of "qualified research" expenses for the tax year over the research expenses for the "base period." (That is generally the three immediately preceding tax years, but there is a phase-in rule.) For an organization conducting research for the first time, the credit may not be available.

"Qualified research" expenses are in-house research expenses, including wages and supplies, plus certain lease and other research equipment charges. These costs must be incurred for "qualified services" (almost everything except work done on government grants and in the areas of social sciences and humanities). Qualified research expenses also include 65% of the amount paid to any person other than an employee. Such amounts may be paid to tax exempt universities, colleges and other research organizations (not private foundations) for basic research pursuant to a written research agreement.

ERTA provides tough rules for qualification so that few, if any, R&D tax shelters, as presently structured, will qualify for the new credit. We're sure before long you'll see the first attempt by shelter sponsors to get around these rules. R&D shelters will continue to benefit from current deduction of expenditures, a new three-year write-off of equipment and lowering of the capital gains tax rate.

3 TO 1 WRITE-OFFS — DON'T TRY 'EM

Year end is the start of silly season for tax shelters, and this year is likely to be worse than usual, since every year end is worse than the year before. It's your last chance to beat income taxes. You'll see plenty of 3 to 1 write-offs, or more. Your conservative accountant says these levels of write-offs are almost impossible to achieve legitimately. You're thinking even if you get audited, you'll just have to pay the taxes due plus interest — no different than a loan from a bank. Wrong!

As we explained earlier, you now effectively pay the prime rate on delinquent taxes with no deduction for interest — a very expensive loan. The new tax law also provides other new penalties that should give you pause for thought. The new rules:

- Interest charges on the amount of any tax underpayment will be equal to 100% of October's prime rate (20% for 1982).
- Non-deductible penalties for negligence or intentional disregard of IRS rules and regulations can be assessed at 5% of the tax underpayment and 50% of the interest due.
- If you claim excessive depreciation or investment tax credit (ITC) because of a "valuation overstatement," you are subject to a non-deductible penalty of as much as 30% of the tax underpayment.
- The new rules and new tax rates triple the cost to you if the IRS disallows big write-offs.

The Background

Say you buy a 3 for 1 shelter (three dollars of advertised tax loss per one dollar of investment) that you know in your heart has little economic merit. In other words, the asset that produces the shelter might not be worth your cash investment. Your motivation in making the investment is the tax loss.

In the past, you had two advantages — you would probably not be audited (there was only a one in ten chance with taxable income over $50,000), and even if you were caught, the cost might not be great. Here are the assumptions: A $10,000 cash investment creates $30,000 of tax losses (you'd have to be on the hook for $20,000 of debt to achieve this result under the so-called "at-risk" rules unless the investment is in real estate); the IRS catches you three years after your return was filed; the investment is worthless, and the tax losses are completely disallowed (because the transaction was not entered into for profit).

Old Rules

Investment Phase

Advertised Tax Loss		$30,000
Assumed Tax Bracket		x 50%
Tax Savings		$15,000
Less: Investment Cost		-10,000
Net Benefit After Tax		$ 5,000

Recapture Phase

Deduction Disallowed		$30,000
Assumed Tax Bracket		x 50%
Tax Underpayment		$15,000
Tax Penalty Due (@ 5%)		750
Interest Due (@ 12% over three years)	$5,400*	
After-Tax Cost	x 50%	
Net Interest Cost		2,700
Total Amount Due in Three Years		$18,450
Total Due Discounted to Present Value (@ 12%)		$13,132
Plus: Investment Value		0
Net Recapture		$13,132

*Deductible

192

If the investment is worthless and you are caught, your net cost is $8,132 ($13,132 of Net Recapture less $5,000 of Net Benefit — see the preceding table). And, if you weren't audited, you made 50% on your investment in one year ($15,000 tax savings versus an investment of $10,000). Your chances of avoiding audit were nine in ten. You can see why people played the game.

The Change

Now the potential net financial cost after tax is $15,820 ($20,820 of Net Recapture less $5,000 of Net Benefit — see the table on the following page), twice the cost under the old law. The potential cost of being nailed is about three times the Net Benefit you receive if you get away with it.

Further, the IRS is attacking abusive shelters (usually defined as transactions with minimal investment merit that promise high tax savings). Your chances of being audited are substantially increased. The IRS is doing everything it can to catch you. (See page 9: "IRS — The Bark and The Bite.") The odds have changed dramatically.

You're better off making a contribution to your favorite charity. A $10,000 gift in 1982 in the 50% bracket would cost you $5,000 versus $15,820 if you are caught with a worthless 3 to 1 write-off deal.

New Rules

Investment Phase

Advertised Tax Loss	$30,000
Assumed Tax Bracket	x 50%
Tax Savings	$15,000
Less: Investment Cost	-10,000
Net Benefit After Tax	$5,000

Recapture Phase

Deduction Disallowed		$30,000
Assumed Tax Bracket		x 50%
Tax Due		$15,000
Tax Penalty Due (@ 5%)		750
Interest Due (@ 20% over three years)	$9,000*	
After-Tax Cost	x 50%	
Net Interest Cost		4,500
Interest Penalty (non-deductible) (50% x $9,000)		4,500
Overvaluation Penalty (30% x $15,000)		4,500
Total Amount Due in Three Years		$29,250
Total Due Discounted to Present Value (@ 12%)		$20,820
Plus: Investment Value		0
Net Recapture		$20,820

*Deductible

EVALUATING RETURNS
FOR TAX SHELTER INVESTMENTS

THE BEST WAY TO COMPARE TAX SHELTER INVESTMENTS

The two toughest problems tax shelter investors face are comparing a particular shelter investment's rate of return to other types of investments and comparing tax shelters to each other. This is difficult for two major reasons. First, there are a number of ways of figuring a tax shelter's rate of return — some of which are misleading. Second, tax shelters are complicated because they provide three kinds of returns: tax savings, cash distributions and capital gains. The rate of return calculations are difficult to make.

Different tax shelter investments have different types of economic benefits which vary in importance and timing. For instance, most if not all of the return of subsidized housing is tax savings. In oil and gas, it's initially tax savings; later, it's cash distributions which are partially tax sheltered by the depletion allowance. With commercial real estate, there's some initial tax savings, a cash flow that may be partially sheltered by depreciation and the eventual possibility of tax-free proceeds from a refinanced mortgage or the profit from a sale at low capital gains rates.

The rate of return from a tax shelter should be looked at qualitatively as well as quantitatively. For example, if you desired cash flow in retirement and received tax savings instead, the savings wouldn't be worth as much if the level of your retirement income put you in a lower tax bracket. Hence, you would not have the type of return you had hoped for.

Of course, the real question is whether the stream of economic benefits has been projected realistically. Just because you are shown financial projections, doesn't mean they will happen as advertised. The assumptions for projections are more important than how the numbers add up.

On the other hand, projections should be made because tax shelters are generally long-term investments. What's more, you should try to analyze the economic benefits so that you can pick a tax shelter that will give you the best kind of return for your needs.

And when you analyze these economic benefits remember that the rate of return of a tax shelter investment is affected by the amount and the timing of the cash you pay in and the economic benefits you receive. Timing is important for this reason: A dollar in hand today is worth more than one in hand tomorrow because it can be invested now and provide you with more than a dollar in the future. All else equal, if two investments require you to pay in the same amount of cash, the one which calls for the least money up front is the least costly. Similarly, the sooner the economic benefits occur, the more valuable they are to you.

To be most useful and accurate, a rate-of-return method must consider this time value. The traditional method is called the Internal Rate of Return ("IRR"). We prefer its near cousin, the Adjusted Rate of Return ("ARR").

In this chapter, we'll give you a step-by-step guide to calculating both measures of return, and we'll show you why the ARR is better. Our examples include actual keystroke instructions for hand-held calculators. The step-by-step approach to calculating returns outlined below has the following advantages:

- Helps you recognize and properly evaluate all the economic benefits from a tax shelter investment;
- Provides an organized procedure for you to follow when making your calculations;
- Focuses on after-tax returns;
- Results in an accurate measure of your investment's true economic returns and;
- If you use a consistent ARR method, you'll be able to compare tax shelters with each other and with alternative securities investments.

The process involved in calculating return is really quite simple once you get used to doing it. From now on, you'll need a pocket calculator which can perform financial functions. We use a Hewlett Packard 12-C or 38-E, or a Texas Instruments TI-59.

Return Calculations Made Easy

STEP ONE — Determine the present value of your investment. You should use the present value of your cash outlay when you examine a tax shelter investment. With some tax shelter investments, the limited partners have to make periodic payments (capital contributions) over several years. The time value of money becomes important. For example, consider these two investments.

	Investment A		Investment B	
Year	Cash	Present Value*	Cash	Present Value*
1982	$ 20,000	$20,000	$ 30,000	$30,000
1983	20,000	18,868	25,000	23,585
1984	20,000	17,800	20,000	17,800
1985	20,000	16,792	15,000	12,594
1986	20,000	15,842	10,000	7,921
TOTAL	$100,000	$89,302	$100,000	$91,900

*At 6% discount rate per annum.

All else being equal, you're better off with the deal that calls for less cash up front (Investment A) even though both transactions require a $100,000 investment. Reason: Investment A's slower pay-in schedule in effect means you have made a smaller investment in present value terms than is required in B. If you had looked at the total capital contributions only, both investments would appear to be the same.

You should always use the present value of your cash outlay when looking at rates of return. The present value is the true cost of the tax shelter commitment. It's the return on this amount you want to track. To determine your true cost (present value of investment), you must discount your future investment pay-ins to present value. We suggest you use a **"safe" after-tax rate** — that is, the after-tax rate you could readily earn on an alternative liquid investment, like the yield on short-term municipal bonds.

To make rates of return comparable, you must use the same safe rate for each investment you look at. And, to make tax shelter rates of return comparable to securities returns, you should use a realistic current market rate as the safe rate.

We will take you through an actual calculation of a real estate investment and show you how to figure rates of return yourself. The investment calls for a pay-in of $20,000 a year for five years. The present value of making this investment is calculated in the table below:

Present Value of Investment

Year	(FV) Cash Paid	(N) Period Paid	(i) Discount Rate	(PV) Present Value
1982	20,000	0	6%	20,000
1983	20,000	1	6%	18,868
1984	20,000	2	6%	17,800
1985	20,000	3	6%	16,792
1986	20,000	4	6%	15,842
TOTAL	100,000			89,302

To make the present value calculation above:

1. Your initial investment is a current cash outlay so the amount of the investment ($20,000 in 1982) is also the present value amount. Enter this number in the first line under the Present Value column.

2. The next investment ($20,000 in 1983) occurs one year later, Period 1. Enter into the calculator the number 20,000; then press "CHS" (Change Sign) button; then press the "FV" (Future Value) button.

3. Enter the period of this 1983 pay-in (the number 1 in this case); then press the "N" (Number of Years) button.

4. Enter the discount rate (the safe rate). We picked six percent. You can choose any rate. Then press the "i" (Percentage Interest Rate) button.

5. Press the "PV" (Present Value) button which will give

you the present value of the second pay-in. Enter the answer, $18,868, in the second line under the Present Value Column.

6. Repeat these steps for each investment pay-in, and then add them up. The present value of the investment, or true cost, is $89,302.

The four calculator functions PV, FV, i, N are connected by a program that calculates the missing function. Enter three functions; then push the button for the missing function and the calculator will produce the missing number.

STEP TWO — Assemble the financial information on the particular tax shelter investment you are considering. The typical private placement memorandum will contain financial projections, or you will have to estimate the shelter's economic benefits yourself. You'll need to know the amount and year of the economic benefits on an after-tax basis. The economic benefits are tax savings (tax loss times your tax bracket), and cash distributions (less any tax due, which is taxable income times your tax bracket) and the proceeds of sale of the shelter after you pay off any debt and pay the taxes (including capital gains taxes) due on the sale.

The lines and columns in the table below are exactly what you need to make the return calculations. Worksheets are provided at the end of this chapter so you can assemble this information conveniently.

Real Estate Investment

Year	Investment Cash Paid-In	Tax Savings (Cost)	Cash Flow	After-Tax Proceeds from Sale of Assets
1982	$ 20,000	$ 8,000	0	0
1983	20,000	17,000	0	0
1984	20,000	19,000	0	0
1985	20,000	9,000	$1,000	0
1986	20,000	8,000	1,000	0
1987	0	7,000	1,000	0
1988	0	5,000	1,000	$103,000
TOTAL	$100,000	$73,000	$4,000	$103,000

Columns under "Summary of Economic Benefits": Tax Savings (Cost), Cash Flow, After-Tax Proceeds from Sale of Assets.

Caution: Do not reduce your yearly investment by tax savings or cash distributions received during the investment pay-in period (the so-called "net investment" method). Tax savings and cash distributions are actually investment returns and should not be used to reduce your investment basis when computing rates of return. Using the erroneous net investment method is like reducing your investment in a bond by the amount of interest you receive periodically. After five or six years of doing that, you'll make the mistake of thinking that you're receiving a very handsome return. Put simply, money you put up is after-tax capital. Investment benefits, such as tax losses, in effect may only be borrowed from Uncle Sam and are not a permanent reduction of investment. They should be viewed as one part of your return. Here's an example:

Investment A

Year	Cash Outlay	Tax Savings	Cash Flow	Net Investment
1982	$ 20,000	$10,000	—	$10,000
1983	20,000	8,000	—	12,000
1984	20,000	6,000	$ 8,000	6,000
1985	20,000	4,000	8,000	8,000
1986	20,000	$ 2,000	8,000	10,000
TOTAL	$100,000	$30,000	$24,000	$46,000

Net investment changes every year. If the $8,000 cash flow continues in the 6th year, the return on the $46,000 net investment would come to 17%. If in the 7th year you made the calculation on the new net investment outstanding of $38,000 at the end of the 6th year, the return would be 21%. Using the concept of net investment to calculate your return is very misleading. Professionals don't use this method of calculating tax shelter returns to make an investment decision, and you shouldn't either.

This misleading net investment concept is often used to calculate rates of return so that high rates can be advertised to prospective tax shelter buyers. Be suspicious when very high return figures are suggested for tax shelter investments.

Let's examine the information in the Summary of Economic Benefits in our real estate example and show you how we derived each of the economic benefits. (See the table below.)

We start with an estimate of tax losses. Tax losses can be used to offset your income from other sources and reduce your tax bill. In the 50% tax bracket each dollar of projected tax losses will result in fifty cents of tax savings for the investor. Remember, if the real estate deal creates taxable income, this will increase your taxes instead of lowering them. If applicable, this tax cost must be included here as a negative number.

This real estate investment generates a cash flow of $1,000 in each of the last four years. This money is assumed to be paid out to you and is an after-tax amount. Cash flow is after tax because all tax consequences were factored into the Taxable Loss (Income) column.

Economic Benefits of the Investment

Year	Taxable Loss (Income)	x	Tax Rate	=	Tax Savings (Cost)	+	Cash Flow	+	After-Tax Proceeds from Sale of Assets	=	Total Economic Benefits
1982	$ 16,000	x	50%	−	$ 8,000	+	0	+	0	=	$ 8,000
1983	34,000	x	50%	=	17,000	+	0	+	0	=	17,000
1984	38,000	x	50%	=	19,000	+	0	+	0	=	19,000
1985	18,000	x	50%	=	9,000	+	$1,000	+	0	=	10,000
1986	16,000	x	50%	=	8,000	+	1,000	+	0	=	9,000
1987	14,000	x	50%	=	7,000	+	1,000	+	0	=	8,000
1988	10,000	x	50%	=	5,000	+	1,000	+	$103,000	=	109,000
	$146,000				$73,000		$4,000		$103,000		$180,000

Note: Assumes benefits are received at the end of each year.

You estimate that the sale of the property at the end of seven years will result in a $160,000 cash distribution to you after the mortgage balance is paid off. This is a before-tax distribution, so you need to deduct taxes due on the sale.

First, you must determine your taxable gain. The quick way is to add the cash you'll receive from the sale (after repayment of any mortgage) to the cumulative tax losses and cash flow for each year you were in the investment. Then, subtract your original cash investment:

Taxable Gain Calculation

Cash from Sale of Property	$160,000
Add:	
Cumulative Tax Loss	+ 146,000
Cumulative Cash Flow	+ 4,000
Less:	
Cash Investment	− 100,000
Taxable Gain	$210,000

Part of the gain may be subject to tax at a 50% tax rate (so-called "recapture"). For instance, the cumulative excess of accelerated depreciation over the straight-line amount for residential property is such an item. The balance of the gain would be a capital gain.

Tax Due Calculation

Recapture:	50% x $ 50,000* =	$25,000
Capital Gain:	20% x $160,000 =	32,000
Total Taxes Due:		$57,000

*The amount is usually supplied in the offering memorandum, or you must estimate it.

Now deduct these taxes due from the pre-tax cash distribution on sale to figure your after-tax cash proceeds of sale.

After-Tax Proceeds of Sale

Cash from Sale of Property	$160,000
Less:	
Taxes Due on Sale	− 57,000
After-Tax Proceeds of Sale	$103,000

Your entire evaluation of an investment's economic merit relies on the accuracy of financial projections. Understand the assumptions which underlie all of these projections, and be sure they are realistic. For real estate deals, you should pay close attention to projected vacancy rates, rental income, operating expenses, financing costs and potential appreciation.

STEP THREE — Calculate the interest you will earn reinvesting the economic benefits as you receive them. Let's say you can reinvest the benefits from the real estate deal in municipal bonds and get an after-tax yield of 6% (back to our old safe-rate concept). Adjust your total economic benefits for each year by compounding them forward to their future value at the end of the investment period, the year you estimate you'll sell the investment. Here's the table:

Adjusted Rate of Return

Year	Economic Benefits (1)(2)	Reinvestment Rate	Number of Reinvestment Periods (3)	Future Value of Economic Benefits
1982	$ 8,000	6%	6	$ 11,348
1983	17,000	6%	5	22,750
1984	19,000	6%	4	23,987
1985	10,000	6%	3	11,910
1986	9,000	6%	2	10,112
1987	8,000	6%	1	8,480
1988	109,000	6%	0	109,000
TOTAL	$180,000			$197,587

(1) From the table Economic Benefits of Investment
(2) If in any year the Economic Benefits are negative, you should discount the amount to Present Value at the safe rate and add this Present Value to the amount of your investment. Some have termed this procedure the "Financial Management Rate of Return".
(3) Assumes benefits are received at the end of each year.

To make the future value calculation:

1. Enter $8,000; then press "CHS" and "PV" on your calculator.
2. Enter six, the safe rate; then press "i".
3. Enter six, the reinvestment period; then press "N." The reinvestment period is the number of years from receipt of the economic benefit until the sale of the investment.
4. Press the "FV" button, and the calculator will then

display $11,348. This is the future value of the 1982 economic benefit taking into account the earnings of reinvesting the benefit until 1988.

5. Calculate the future value of each year's economic benefit by following Steps 1 through 4: and then add them up. The total future value is $197,587 in our example.

STEP FOUR — Calculate the Adjusted Rate of Return. The ARR is the rate that equates the total future value of the economic benefits to the present value of the investment — your rate of return. To calculate the ARR:

1. Enter the present value of the investment pay-in from step one ($89,302 in our example); press the "CHS" button; then press the "PV" button.
2. Enter seven (the number of years the investment was held); then press the "N" button.
3. Enter $197,587 (the total future value); then press the "FV" button.
4. Press the "i" button. The ARR is 12.01%, the compound rate of return on your investment assuming reinvestment of benefits at 6%. In other words, if you invest $89,302 at a rate of 12.01% compounded annually, you would have received $197,587 after seven years.

Calculating Internal Rate Of Return

The Internal Rate of Return is the discount rate which equates the yearly economic benefits to the present value of the investment.

The calculator will figure the IRR in a few quick steps. Using the Hewlett Packard 12-C or 38-E (the steps on the Texas Instrument TI-59 are slightly different), the following steps should be performed:

1. Enter present value of the original investment. Press 89,302, then CHS and g CFO.
2. Enter the yearly economic benefits from the earliest to the latest. Press 8,000, then g Cfj.
3. Repeat step (2) for each yearly benefit in order.
4. Press f, then IRR. After several minutes of calculating, the machine will display the IRR which is 14.3678%.

The following table shows that if you discount each year's Economic Benefits using the IRR, the total present value of those benefits will be equal to your initial investment of $89,302.

Internal Rate of Return

Year	Total Economic Benefits	Period	Present Value Rate (IRR)	Present Value Amount
1982	$ 8,000	1	14.4%	$ 6,995
1983	17,000	2	14.4	12,997
1984	19,000	3	14.4	12,701
1985	10,000	4	14.4	5,845
1986	9,000	5	14.4	4,600
1987	8,000	6	14.4	3,575
1988	109,000	7	14.4	42,589
TOTAL	$180,000			$89,302

NOTE: Actual internal rate of return used before rounding is 14.3678%.

Comparing ARR to IRR

We believe the Adjusted Rate of Return (ARR) is the best measure to use when comparing tax shelter investments to each other or when comparing shelters to other types of investments such as stocks or bonds. In fact, it can be employed to analyze any stream of economic benefits. We consider ARR the cornerstone of return analysis for tax shelters.

The primary difference between the ARR and the IRR is the assumed "safe" rate of reinvestment. In ARR, you decide what your safe reinvestment rate is. The IRR assumes that you can reinvest your economic benefits at a yield equal to the IRR. The higher your investment's IRR, the higher the assumed yield you must earn on the economic benefits as you receive them to achieve the IRR. So, the IRR tends to overstate the true economic benefits of an investment. For example, if you compound the original investment ($89,302) at the IRR (14.4%), you end up with $228,553 — an amount far greater than the actual total economic benefits of $197,587.

Another problem is that an investment with an 18% IRR does not provide 50% higher economic benefits than one with a 12% IRR — because the higher IRR assumes reinvestment at a higher rate. The IRR method suggests unrealistically that an investor will face very different reinvestment opportunities depending on the investment he selects.

The IRR represents the rate of return of capital and the rate of return on capital — like a mortgage constant, not a bond yield. So, IRR's are higher than and not comparable to securities yields.

The Internal Rate of Return can be used to compare two very similar investments so long as the assumptions are the same for both calculations, and you understand that the rate determined is not comparable with investment returns as you think of them for stocks and bonds.

If we assumed a 14.4% "safe" reinvestment rate in our example, the ARR would also be 14.4%. This pinpoints the fundamental difference between these two measures — the IRR assumes that the reinvestment rate is equal to the rate of return earned on the investment you are evaluating; the ARR allows you to choose a more realistic reinvestment rate.

Alternative Methods

Another way to compare similar investments is to calculate the Present Value Per Dollar Invested. You do that by dividing the sum of the present values of an investment's economic benefits by the present value of the amount invested. Look at the following table:

Year	Economic Benefits (1)	Reinvestment Rate	Number of Reinvestment Periods (2)	Present Value of Economic Benefits
1982	$ 8,000	6%	1	$ 7,547
1983	17,000	6%	2	15,130
1984	19,000	6%	3	15,953
1985	10,000	6%	4	7,921
1986	9,000	6%	5	6,725
1987	8,000	6%	6	5,639
1988	109,000	6%	7	72,491
TOTAL	$180,000			$131,406
ORIGINAL INVESTMENT				÷ $ 89,302
PRESENT VALUE PER DOLLAR INVESTED				= 1.47

(1) From the table Economic Benefits of Investment.
(2) Assumes benefits received at the end of each year.

Since the Present Value Per Dollar Invested is greater than one, this investment's return is greater than a 6% municipal bond. Reason: We discounted the investment's economic benefits at the rate of 6%. The one drawback for purposes of comparison is that the Present Value Per Dollar Invested is a ratio. Hence, it's difficult to relate the result to the investment returns of securities. On the other hand, you can still use this method for comparative analysis of similar investments. The higher the ratio the better the return.

Other Factors

Partitioning the rate of return and probability analysis are now becoming popular in evaluating returns, too. Partitioning (separating the return attributable to each individual economic benefit) is useful in comparing investments. It also helps to determine whether an investment's benefits are suitable for a particular investor and what factors are most important to investigate.

In the table below, economic benefits are separated as follows: tax savings - 45%; cash flow - 2%; and sale proceeds - 53%. Sale proceeds, since they represent such a large component of the total return, become the most important assumption to investigate.

Future Value at 6%

Year	Tax Savings	Cash Flow	Sale Proceeds	Economic Benefits
1982	$11,348	—	—	$ 11,348
1983	22,750	—	—	22,750
1984	23,987	—	—	23,987
1985	10,719	$1,191	—	11,910
1986	8,989	1,123	—	10,112
1987	7,420	1,060	—	8,480
1988	5,000	1,000	$103,000	109,000
TOTAL	$90,213	$4,374	$103,000	$197,587
PERCENTAGE	45%	2%	53%	100%

Probability analysis can be used to examine the likelihood that economic benefits will occur. That, in turn, will give you a more exact rate of return calculation or a range of possible returns.

In addition, there are many other helpful measures of return that can be used to check-out tax shelter investments — cash on cash return, payback period, net future revenues and so on. However, these are only useful for comparing similar investments.

The Adjusted Rate of Return method can be used effectively to compare tax shelter investments. And, you can use it to compare tax shelter returns to securities returns. This method is the investor's most reliable mathematical yardstick in evaluating investment alternatives. As a broad generalization, the ARR should fall within a 9% to 12% range after tax for most acceptable, investment-grade tax shelters (assuming a 6% reinvestment rate).

The Stanger Rate-of-Return Calculation Worksheet

The following pages show you how to calculate rates of return for tax shelter investments. Our easy to follow step-by-step instruction sheets set forth keystroke instructions for use with Hewlett Packard hand-held calculators. We show both Adjusted Rate of Return and Internal Rate of Return calculations, so you'll be able to compare tax shelter investments by both rate-of-return methods.

Present Value of Investment

Year	Cash Paid [FV]	Period Date [N]	Safe Rate [i]	Present Value of Investment [PV]
	$	0	%	$
		1		
		2		
		3		
		4		
		5		
		6		
		7		
		8		
TOTAL	$			$

Rate-of-Return Calculation Worksheet (continued)
Value of Economic Benefits

Year	Taxable Loss (Income)	× Tax Rate	= Tax Savings (Cost)	+ Cash Flow	+ After-Tax Proceeds From Sale of Asset	= Total Economic Benefits (1) [PV]	Safe Rate [i]	Periods Until Sale [N]	Adjusted Future Value of Economic Benefits [FV]
	$		$	$	$	$	%		$
TOTAL	$		$	$	$	$	%		$

(1) If a number in this column is negative, discount the amount back to Present Value and add to the Present Value of Investment.

Rate-of-Return
Calculation Instructions

Step One — Determine the Present Value of Your Investment.

1. Your initial investment is a current cash outlay so the amount of the investment is also the present value amount. Enter this number in the first line under Cash Paid as well as under the column "Present Value of Investment" on the form on page 211.
2. List on the form each subsequent investment pay-in in the period in which it occurs.
3. Enter into the calculator the amount of the second investment pay-in. Press the "CHS" (Change Sign) button; then press the "FV" (Future Value) button.
4. Enter the number of the period in which this investment is paid; then press the "N" (Number of Periods) button.
5. Enter the discount rate (the safe rate); then press the "i" (Percentage Interest Rate) button.
6. Press the "PV" (Present Value) button which will give you the present value of the second pay-in. Enter the answer in the second line under the Present Value Column.
7. Repeat Steps 3 through 6 for each investment pay-in and then add them up. The total is the present value of the investment.

STEP TWO — Determine the Economic Benefits of the Investment.

1. List the investment's projected Taxable Loss (Income) for each year; then multiply by your assumed tax rate. The result is the amount of Tax Savings per year.
2. Add the investment's projected Tax Savings, Cash Flow and After-Tax Proceeds for each year. The sum is the investment's Total Economic Benefits per year. Enter these amounts in the first several columns on the worksheet on page 212. For real estate investments the After-Tax Proceeds are calculated as follows: Cash from Sale of Property plus Cumulative Tax Loss and

Instructions (continued)

Cumulative Cash Flow less Cash Investment equals Taxable Gain. Calculate Taxes Due on Sale. Subtract Taxes Due on Sale from Cash from Sale of Property to find After-Tax Sales Proceeds.

STEP THREE — Calculate the Adjusted Future Value of Economic Benefits.

1. Enter the amount of the first year's Economic Benefit; press the "CHS" button; then press the "PV" button.
2. Enter the safe rate, then press "i."
3. Enter the Reinvestment Period, then press "N." The Reinvestment Period is the number of years from receipt of the Economic Benefit until the sale of the investment. If you are estimating the sale of an investment seven years after the first pay-in of original investment, the Reinvestment Period will be six years for an Economic Benefit received in the second period. The second period can be the same year as the year of original investment.
4. Press the "FV" button and the calculator will then display the future value of the first economic benefit taking into account the earnings of reinvesting the benefit at the "safe" rate until the investment is sold. This is the Adjusted Future Value of Economic Benefits.
5. Calculate the future value of each year's Economic Benefit by following Steps 1 through 4, and then add them up.

STEP FOUR — Calculate the Adjusted Rate of Return.

1. Enter the total Present Value of Investment from Step One; press the "CHS" button; then press the "PV" button.
2. Enter the number of years the investment was held; then press the "N" button.
3. Enter the total Adjusted Future Value of Economic Benefits; then press the "FV" button.
4. Press the "i" button. The machine will then calculate the Adjusted Rate of Return, the compound rate of return on your investment assuming reinvestment of benefits at the "safe" rate.

Instructions (continued)

STEP FIVE — Calculate the Internal Rate of Return.

1. Enter the total Present Value of Investment from Step One. Then press (in order) the buttons, CHS and g CFO.
2. Enter the first yearly Economic Benefit; then press the button g Cfj.
3. Repeat Step Two for each Economic Benefit in order from the first one received to the last.
4. Press f, then IRR. After several minutes of calculating, the machine will display the IRR.

SHELTER OUTLOOK

TAX SHELTERS — ALIVE AND WELL

Remember the saying, "a bear market is when stocks return to their rightful owners?" I really believe that's what's happening in both the real estate and oil and gas business. This year should go down as a tremendous buying opportunity — ironically just when tax shelter sales are experiencing the first big drop in a decade. Real estate and oil and gas have tremendous appeal on a longer term basis with or without inflation.

I must say, I thought the tax shelter game showed signs of weariness last fall when my piano teacher (no kidding!) asked me what I thought of that "hot, new R&D deal, Trilogy? I put $5,000 in and I sure hope it works," he said, glad to be in the ranks of those for whom a "tax shelter" was an appropriate investment. Is that a market top or is that a market top?

Mix the coming economic reality, lower inflation, with the expert salesman's pitch for tax shelters, and you can see why sales of tax shelters are falling. To wit: "The two most insidious and destructive forces attacking your net worth and economic survival are taxes and inflation." The average investor isn't so sure taxes (remember the hoped-for bracket reductions in the Economic Recovery Tax Act of 1981) or inflation are such great negatives as they were just six months ago. The result in the first quarter of 1982 has been the most precipitous decline in tax shelter programs sales in recent memory. For instance, oil and gas drilling program sales were off 38% from the average quarter of 1981.

Because it's been a one-way street for so long, everyone thought the tax shelter business was immune to cycles. But, fluctuations are a fact of economic life. Apparently, disinflation is "in" and inflation is a factor only in banana Republics, not in this great land of ours. My, how fickle are the basic fears of the investing public.

Likely, it's no coincidence this slackening of activity matches a decline in the selling price of single family homes, a drop in the wholesale price index and a reduction in the price of gasoline at the pump. The former and the latter are the most obvious components of the "price index" to large segments of the public. Wholesale prices are, after all, the most obvious indicator to the businessman or entrepreneur who are the backbone of the traditional tax shelter market.

If I've ever seen a trend overdone or overextended, it was the one on the way up. Wall Street quadrupled the amount of money raised for tax shelters from 1979 to 1981. You know it doesn't matter what era, generation, economy or business you're talking about, growing at that pace can't be managed successfully. Marketing was king — sell the sizzle not the steak. All else was a support function. Product won out over prudence and guess what? The over-eager buyers will suffer a little. Not all investments are destined to work out.

Now, I think I'm witnessing a trend being badly overdone on the downside. Investor perception and objective reality are poles apart. (More about this later.) Confusion over new tax rules and the economic rationale for so-called tax shelter investments are taking their toll on the spirits of the purveyors and the pocketbooks of the purchasers. Both good and bad investments are being ignored — the world's broadest brush is brushing again (isn't that how it goes?), always a sure sign of the bottom. Business is grinding to a slow walk. But, let's look at the facts.

Tax shelters are the classic hedge against the current uncertainties of federal government policy. Say Reaganomics works, business booms, interest rates keep declining and further tax cuts are in the offering. Income-producing assets will earn more and be worth more. Deferring current income to later years when tax rates will be lower is a sensible strategy. On the other hand, let's say Congress can't restrain spending, huge federal budget deficits proliferate and taxes increase. You'll need tax shelters more than ever.

Tax shelter investing looks appealing whichever scenario you favor. Heads or tails, you win. How about the underlying economics?

First, real estate. Rents today for most types of real estate average far less than the rent levels necessary to pay a fair return on today's construction cost. The result — a huge increase in rents is coming, and that means a huge increase in cash flows, and probably in real estate values. See the chapter "Apartments as Investments" for the extraordinary opportunity represented by investing in apartments today.

The large insurance companies will put up 100% of the construction cost of a property and accept a 9% to 12% fixed return on this cash investment, well below competitive returns today. The kicker? They will also take (earn) one-half the increases in cash flow from operations and one-half the net proceeds when the property is refinanced or sold. See where they are putting their bet? On the future. And at a pretty fair sacrifice of rate for the funds they advance today. That shows where their convictions lie.

Real estate is the major beneficiary of the Economic Recovery Tax Act of 1981. The new tax laws provide major new breaks for real estate ownership, from faster write-offs to rehabilitation tax credits. The depreciation rules even portend fewer arguments with the IRS over tax shelter deductions. Buying existing commercial property is particularly attractive now from a tax standpoint.

And for oil and gas, the outlook is also bullish. Worldwide hydrocarbon reserves are declining. The rate at which we are producing oil and gas exceeds the amount added to reserves annually from new wells. Just to prevent a decline in worldwide reserves, two Prudhoe Bays or one North Sea would have to be discovered each year. But, the last field of this size popped up in 1969.

And, what if Iran moves a little west then turns left? Do you know where Kuwait and Saudi Arabia are?

Sure, we've conserved, recessed and parked. The result is to leave the residual suppliers, OPEC, with a 4 to 6 million barrel-a-day production capacity above current worldwide consumption levels, the so-called glut. To put the glut in perspective, a return to 1979 consumption levels in the U.S. alone would all but wipe out the current excess capacity worldwide.

Forgetting speculation, drilling funds at this time seem particularly attractive for many other reasons. For one thing, the domestic U.S. hydrocarbon plays have been predominantly natural gas, not oil, in recent years. Hydrocarbon reserves of drilling funds are estimated to be 65% natural gas. Natural gas is selling at about one-half the price of oil on an energy equivalency basis, thanks to price controls. Some gas (tite, Devonian, deep) is allowed free market prices or prices much higher than for controlled gas. The price of gas can rise while the price of oil declines.

For another, it's a buyer's market, and that's a dramatic switch from last year. Prospects and farm-ins are cheaper, better and more prolific. The cost of supplies and rigs is declining. This translates to better economics, lower risks and higher net revenue interests. I'd rather buy now than at any time in the last two years. Most people in the "oil patch" feel the same way.

The change is the most incredible I've ever seen since 1973. You want drill pipe? You can buy some from every operator — you don't need to call the manufacturer. Apparently, there's about a one-year's supply in inventory (probably an exaggeration but not by much). You want to rent a rig? How many, how soon and how much will you pay per foot (day rates are remembered nostalgically). In most areas you can rent rigs at considerable discounts from last year's rates.

You're looking for leases, prospects, acreage blocks, acquisitions, joint ventures or participations in wells (even spudded or in the completion phase)? Raise your hand — your plate will be full quicker than you can fry an egg. The big companies expanded too fast and budgets are overextended. The little companies played the game on credit and have been brutalized by high interest rates.

But, the profit potential per barrel is very high by historic standards. Even at a $31 per barrel selling price, operating costs plus local and windfall profit taxes are about $7 per barrel, leaving $24 in your pocket. Drilling and development costs were estimated at $13 per barrel for the industry in 1981 for a profit of about $11 a barrel. The comparative profit number in 1973 was probably 75 cents per barrel. Higher profits per barrel net of drilling costs means high profits in drilling for oil and gas today.

In the drilling program business, there's a definite trend toward better deals for the limited partner. Two reasons are apparent. One is competition for the investor's cash. The other is sponsor realization the investor needs a fair shake to keep coming back to the window. In many deals now, the general partner shares pre-case point risk with the limited partner (the so-called "promoted interest" structure, unheard of formerly) and/or only "promotes" the limited partner on the first well on a prospect. Subsequent wells are drilled "straight up" — each partner's share of costs is equal to his share of revenues.

Finally, the new tax legislation is better for oil and gas investors, not worse (also true for most other "tax shelter" investments including real estate). Lower tax brackets slightly reduce tax losses but greatly increase after-tax income. The net result favors the investor. The investors' perception is that lower tax brackets kill tax shelters. The reality is exactly the opposite.

1982 TAX LEGISLATION AND SHELTER INVESTMENTS

THE IMPACT OF 'TEFRA' ON TAX SHELTERS

There's bad news for the post-Labor Day, year-end, deep shelter mania in the new tax act (the Tax Equity and Fiscal Responsibility Act!! of 1982) — the penalties are large for getting caught in abusive shelters (those solely motivated by tax avoidance), and the IRS can go after investors more easily now than ever before. These particular changes are effective immediately so you should invest more conservatively in tax shelters for the rest of 1982.

Surprisingly, other changes, for instance in the so-called "individual minimum tax," make tax shelters more attractive for most investors. And luckily, there are no detrimental provisions or significant changes in the new tax rules affecting legitimate tax shelters.

Other provisions generally make it much tougher to avoid reporting taxable income from dividends, interest and capital gains. In fact, these new reporting and compliance provisions are estimated to increase federal tax collections by more than $30 billion dollars over the next three years, a positive stimulus to tax shelter sales.

Here is the list of the new income reporting provisions in the tax act that will influence the reporting of substantial amounts of previously unreported income:

- Effective July 1, 1983, witholding at the rate of 10% is required on payments of dividends and interest. (There are exemptions when amounts are small.) Effectively, registration is required for ownership of all debt obligations offered by corporations and the United States and its agencies (over one year maturity). There are no more bearer bonds except U.S. Treasuries.

- The new tax bill permits the IRS to require information returns from stockbrokers on gross proceeds of sales for customers (not to be effective before January 1, 1983).
- Information returns must be filed for taxpayers with state or local tax refunds.

The capital gains tax has not yet been changed. But, a provision to reduce the holding period for long-term capital gains to six months has been added to a minor debt limit bill now before the Senate. Sales or exchanges after June 30, 1982 would be affected by this shorter holding period if the bill becomes law.

The new law reduces slightly the favorable impact of the regular investment tax credit and the energy and historic real estate rehabilitation tax credits and is generally effective for assets placed in service after December 31, 1982. You will be required to reduce the depreciable cost "basis" of the asset by 50% of the amount of the credit. Alternatively, for regular investment tax credit property only you may elect a 2% reduction in the amount of the credit (say, from 10% to 8%) and not have to make the "basis" adjustment. Finally, you may only reduce with investment credits 85% of income tax liability in excess of $25,000 versus 90% before. The new rules will have a negligible impact on tax shelter investments.

The new law repeals the increases in ACRS deductions which were scheduled to begin in 1985. Under ERTA, depreciation was to be based upon the 150% declining balance method through 1984, changing to 175% in 1985 and 200% thereafter. TEFRA eliminates these changes and makes the 150% rate permanent.

The new law eliminates nearly all of the differences between corporate and non-corporate qualified retirement plans. Contribution limits are decreased (as are benefits) for corporate plans, and there are new restrictions on borrowing from plans. The IRS is permitted to disregard the corporate tax status of personal service corporations. You may want to liquidate a personal service corporation if you own one. The new inclusion of pension assets over $100,000 in your estate for tax purposes (no more annuity exemptions) will require new estate plans for some individuals. The rules are effective for tax years beginning in 1983.

The method of calculating the interest charge on delinquent taxes will change. The new rate will be based on the average prime rate during the six months preceding September 30th and March 30th and will become effective the following January 1st and July 1st respectively. The current 20% charge will apply until January 1, 1983 at which time the six-month average ended September 30th will become effective.

Abusive Shelters

The IRS has a new and powerful tool to attack abusive tax shelters, perhaps the most important change in partnership tax proceedings in a decade — the tax treatment of any partnership item can now be determined at the partnership level rather than in separate proceedings with the partners. This new procedure seems to allow the IRS to go after shelters, not taxpayers, and allows wholesale disallowance of what the IRS considers questionable tax losses. This approach should reduce the backlog in Tax Court and bring tax loss issues to a final determination much earlier. It's a reiteration of the trend of recent tax legislation toward making the "audit lottery" more like Russian Roulette.

Abusive shelters are the target of several other new provisions which are effective immediately. Promoters, or sellers, of interests in a partnership are subject to new civil penalties where false or fraudulent material shows the availability of tax benefits or where valuation overstatements exceed 200% of the correct value. Real or personal property is frequently assigned unreasonably high values in abusive tax shelters to show inflated depreciation deductions and tax credits. The U.S. can seek to enjoin persons from organizing and selling abusive tax shelters who are engaged in conduct subject to the civil penalty.

If you flirt with the grey areas of the law you better do so with your eyes open. A new 10% non-deductible penalty will be imposed on the amount of a "substantial understatement" of income tax. For understatement due to tax shelter losses, the penalty may be avoided only if you establish you have "substantial authority" for your position and you reasonably believe that the tax treatment claimed is more likely than not the proper treatment for the item. As a tax shelter investor, you will be held to a higher standard of sophistication than others with respect to losses on your return.

Individual Minimum Tax

The important news — for most tax shelter situations the new changes will increase net tax savings from tax shelters. The new alternative minimum tax will not usually come into play. The new alternative minimum tax is a problem if tax shelter losses from preference items are mixed with substantial long-term capital gains or with large differences between the fair market value and the exercise price of qualified stock options. Under these two circumstances, the new alternative minimum tax can reduce the amount of tax shelter that is suitable for you by as much as one-third.

The so-called "preference tax" for individuals, or the 15% add-on minimum tax on tax preference items, is repealed in 1983. Major tax preference items (not an all inclusive list) in tax shelters are: accelerated depreciation on real and personal property in excess of straight line depreciation; intangible drilling costs in excess of net income from production and in excess of the amount otherwise amortizable; depletion allowance in excess of tax basis on oil and gas properties; and two newly added tax preferences — mining exploration and development costs, and research and development costs in excess of normally amortizable amounts.

You will benefit from the elimination of the preference tax if you are a tax shelter investor, as shown in the following example. With $180,000 of gross income and $80,000 of preference item tax shelter losses under the old rules, you would have paid about $9,000 of "preference tax." Net tax savings from the shelter loss would have been reduced from $40,000 to $31,000. But beginning in 1983, the "preference cost" will be eliminated. Put simply, tax shelter tax savings will most likely be the same as your marginal tax bracket.

The "alternative minimum tax" is calculated a new way in 1983. You add tax preference items plus 60% of long-term capital gains and the excess of the fair market value over the exercise price for qualified stock options to adjusted gross income (taxable income plus itemized deductions). Then subtract charitable contributions, medical expenses in excess of 10% of adjusted gross income, casualty losses in excess of 10% of adjusted gross income, personal housing interest and other interest to the extent of net investment income. The first $30,000 of AMT income is not taxed for single returns, $40,000 for joint returns. The remainder is subject to the alternative minimum tax which is levied at the new flat rate of 20%. You calculate your regular tax due and your alternative minimum tax and pay the higher amount. The new alternative minimum tax will not affect most tax shelter buyers.

INDEX

Abusive tax shelters, 9, 10, 11, 193
Accelerated Cost Recovery System (ACRS), 92, 180-187
  anti-churning rules, 182
  commercial and residential property, 92, 93, 186
  comparison with old rules, 94, 95, 142-145, 167-169
  equipment leasing, 165, 166, 188
  subsidized housing, 139, 186
  thoroughbred horses, 174
Adjusted Rate of Return (ARR) 198-210
  comparison with IRR, 207
  how to calculate, 199-206
  see also "Rates of Return"
Alternative minimum tax 15, 46, 180
Anti-churning rules, 182
Apartments
  cash flow and income statements, 85, 86
  condominium conversions of, 120, 126
  construction costs, 106
  demand for, 119, 122, 123
  disappearances, 120
  ERTA's impact, 125
  investment characteristics, 126
  public partnerships, 125-127
  rent levels, 106, 119, 123-124
  vacancy rates, 106
  vs. single-family housing affordability, 123, 124
At-risk rules
  see "Multiple write-offs"
Audits, 9-10
  abusive tax shelters, 9, 10
  how to avoid, 10
  partnership audit ratio, 10
  targets of, 9, 39

Bargain repurchase offer, 134

Capital gains tax rate, 147, 180
Capitalization rate, 98, 101
Carried interest oil and gas program, 68
"Carve-outs", 136
Cash flow
  calculation of, 86, 87, 99
  in net leases, 137
  in real estate, 83, 87
Cash-on-cash return, 111
Certified historic structures
  ERTA's impact on, 139, 143, 145, 186, 187
  rehabilitation of, 139
Commercial property
  see "Real estate investments"
Commodity straddles, 8, 188, 189
Comparing tax shelter investments, 197-210
  see also "Rates of return"
Condominiums, 120, 123, 126
Construction costs
  apartment buildings, 106
  office buildings, 108
  shopping centers, 107
Construction period risks, 109
Controlled wildcat drilling, 63

Deal terms in oil and gas investments, 46
Debt
  calculating taxes due, 26-28
  relief from and taxation, 25-28
  see also "Taxable gain"
Deferred fees in net leases, 136
Depletion allowance, 21, 54, 55, 73, 157
Depreciation
  see "ACRS" and "ERTA"

233

Disclaimers in offering
  memoranda, 31
Distribution agreement shelter, 153
Diversification
  in apartment investments, 116,
    126
  measures of, 62
  reducing risk, 16
Drilling
  developmental, 34, 63
  exploratory, 34, 63
Drilling costs, 5, 51, 222
  deduction of, 19, 20
  sharing of, 61, 62, 64
Drilling programs,
  see "Oil and gas investments"
Due diligence
  defined, 31
  in oil and gas, 33
  in real estate, 35
  objectives of, 31

Economic climate and tax shelters,
  3-8, 219-223
Economic Recovery Tax Act of
  1981 (ERTA), 179-190
  ACRS, 92, 139, 147, 180-184
  alternative minimum tax, 180
  capital gains tax, 180
  comparison with old law, 145
  depreciation of personal
    property, 180, 181, 182
  depreciation of real property,
    125, 147, 182, 183, 184
  depreciation of thoroughbred
    horses, 174, 175
  impact on:
    commodity straddles, 188
    equipment leasing, 165, 166,
      187
    new construction, 139, 141,
      143, 145
    oil and gas, 55-57, 187
    real estate, 84, 91, 139-144,
      147-148, 185-187, 221

    rehabilitation projects, 139,
      140, 142, 143, 145
    R & D shelters, 190
    securities dealers shelters,
      189-190
    subsidized housing, 139, 140-145
    investment tax credits, 184
    tax rates, 179-180
    underpayment penalties, 185,
      191-193
Equipment leasing shelters, 7,
  165-169
  calculation of tax benefits,
    167-169
  depreciation under ACRS, 165,
    167-168
  impact of ERTA, 165-169
  interest rates, 7
  investment tax credits, 166
  safe harbour rules, 166, 187

Foreclosure and taxable gain, 23-26
Franchise agreement shelters, 153
Functional allocation oil and gas
  programs, 61, 62, 67, 68
Futures contracts
  see "Commodity straddles"

Gas wells, economics of, 52
Ground lease, 136

Homestake fraud, 47

Income Funds
  see "Oil and gas income funds"
Income Properties
  see "Real estate investments"
Inflation and tax shelters, 8, 219,
  220
Intangible Drilling Costs
  see "Drilling costs"
Interest rates and tax shelters, 7,
  219
Internal Rate of Return (IRR), 198
  comparison with ARR, 207
  how to calculate, 206-207
  see also "Rates of return"

234

Internal Revenue Service (IRS)
  abusive tax shelters, 9-12, 193
  at-risk rules, 44
  audit selection criteria, 10, 11, 43
  current targets, 9, 39, 43
  R & D partnership rulings, 155
  revenue rulings, 10
  thoroughbred horses, 174
  underpayment penalties, 185, 191-194
Investment Tax Credit (ITC), 7, 184-185
  at-risk rules, 188
  for certified historic rehabs, 7, 186
  for equipment leasing, 166, 188
  in subchapter-S corporations, 184
  with non-recourse debt, 184
ITC shelters, 41

"Legal loan to value" ratio, 97
Leveraged real estate, 79, 81
  see also "Real estate investments"
Licensing agreement shelters, 153
Liquidity and tax shelters, 13, 16, 117, 147
Long-term capital gains tax, 180

Mortgage constant, 101
Multiple write-offs, 41, 83
  and IRS, 43
  at-risk rules, 44, 83

National Association of Securities Dealers (NASD)
  equipment leasing, 7
  liquidity, 117
  professional fees, 40
Natural Gas
  economics of drilling, 5
  Natural Gas Policy Act of 1978, 52, 54

Negative leverage in real estate, 7
Net Investment Ranking, 159-160
  for oil and gas income funds, 161
  method of calculation, 160-161
Net leases, 15, 35, 110-111, 133-136
  deferred fees, 136
  determining benefits of, 137-138
  investor cautions, 135-137
  rate of return from, 138
Net worth, building of, 19
  with oil and gas, 19-21
  with subsidized housing, 22-24
New construction
  see "Real estate investments"
Non-recourse debt, 25, 27, 33, 97, 154, 184
Non-securities offering, 40

Offering document, 31
  absence of, 40
  conflicts of interest, 32
  disclaimers in, 31
  prior activities section, 41
  requesting information, 32
Office buildings
  construction, vacancy and rental data, 109
  see also "Net leases"
Oil and gas income funds, 157-163
  defined, 157
  evaluating deal terms, 159-161
  factors influencing returns, 162-163
  net investment ranking of largest funds, 161
  returns available, 158, 159
Oil and gas investments
  amount at risk, 57
  building net worth with, 19-21
  cash distributions, 21, 22
  cash distribution tables, 60-61
  comparison with stocks, 75
  cost sharing in, 61, 64
  deal structures and terms, 67-71, 223

depletion allowance, 21
diversification, 62
drilling costs, see "Drilling costs"
ERTA, 55-57, 187, 223
economic environment, 4-5, 51
evaluating performance records and success ratios, 59, 60, 63
income funds, see "Oil and gas income funds"
investigation of, 33-34
investment guidelines, 63-65
outlook, 221-223
returns, 55-56, 73-75
revenue sharing, 64, 65
tax deductions, 19, 20, 62, 64, 65
Oil and gas reserves
value of, 21, 158-159
Oil prices
decontrol of, 5
outlook, 52, 162, 222
OPEC, 53, 221
Operational period risks in real estate development, 110
Options straddles, 8, 188-189

Partnership audit ratio, 10
Penalties, see "Tax underpayment penalties"
Private placements
checklist for, 39
illegal solicitation of, 39
memorandum, 31, 32
Professional review fees vs. commissions, 40
Promoted interest oil and gas programs, 61, 68
Prospectus
see "Offering document"

Rates of return, 47, 55, 197-210
adjusted rate of return, 198-210
internal rate of return, 206, 207
of net leases, 138
of oil & gas programs, 75

of subsidized housing, 144
partitioning returns, 209
worksheets and instructions, 211-215
Reagan Administration
legislation affecting apartments, 120
legislation affecting subsidized housing, 140
tax legislation, 12
Real estate investments
advantage of fixed costs, 79-82
apartments, see "Apartments"
appreciation of, 83, 87-88, 130
building net worth, 22-24
calculating benefits of, 83-89
calculating required rents, 102-103, 105
calculating value of, 98-105, 129
cash flows, 79, 89
commercial property, 111, 114
construction costs, 104, 106-108
current trends, 129-131, 221
depreciation, see "Accelerated Cost Recovery System"
determining prices, 121
ERTA's impact on, 91, 139-144, 147-148, 185-187, 221
equity build up, 83, 87
leveraged, 79, 81
multiple write-offs, 44, 83
net leases, see "Net leases"
rent levels, see "Rent levels"
risks, 109-111
subsidized housing, see "Subsidized housing"
tax losses, 83, 88
Real estate publicly registered partnerships, 109, 125-127
investigating, 35-37
investor costs, 114
reasons to invest in, 115-117
Recapture, 45, 147, 166, 168, 183
avoiding, 45, 92
calculating, 87-88, 204
Red-herring, 31

236

Rehabilitation
  ERTA's impact on, 139, 143, 145, 186-187
  of certified historic structures, 139
Rent levels, 79, 106-108, 123-125, 221
Rent-up period risks, 110
Replacement costs, 8, 23, 130
Research and development partnerships
  advantages for inventor, 156
  advantages for investor, 155, 156
  defined, 153, 154
  DeLorean motor car, 153
  ERTA's impact on, 190
  Lear Fan Jet, 153
  license, franchise, distribution agreement shelters, 153, 154
  tax aspects, 154
  Trilogy, Ltd., 153
Residual value fee, 149
Re-syndication, 139, 141, 185
Revenue Act of 1978, 15, 83
Revenue rulings, 10
Reversionary interest oil and gas programs, 60, 67, 68
Review fees, 40
Royalties, 153, 155, 156

Safe harbour provisions, 35, 36, 166, 187
"Section 8" Program
  see "Subsidized housing"
"Section 102" gas, 52
Section 167(k) Rehabilitations, 140, 142-143, 186
Securities dealers shelters, 189, 190
Securities Exchange Commission (SEC), 32, 40, 42
  criteria for suitable shelter investors, 13
  non-securities offering, 40
  offering documents, 31
Semi-proven drilling, 63

Shopping Centers
  construction, vacancy, and rental data, 107
"Stepped-up basis" rules, 16
Straddles
  see "Commodity straddles"
Subsidized housing, 15, 35, 139-141
  building net worth with, 22-24
  defined, 22, 140
  depreciation under ACRS, 142, 143, 145
  determining worth, 23
  impact of ERTA, 139-145
  sale of older projects advised, 147-150

Tangible drilling costs, 20, 64
  see also "Drilling costs"
Tax Equity and Fiscal Responsibility Act of 1982 (TEFRA), 227-231
  abusive shelters, 229
  ACRS deductions, 228
  add-on minimum tax, 230
  alternative minimum tax, 230-231
  income reporting provisions, 227
  interest on delinquent taxes, 229
  investment tax credits, 228
  retirement plans, 228
Tax losses and shelter selection, 25, 43, 83
Tax preference items, 16, 91, 141
Tax rate schedules, 179, 180
Tax Reform Act of 1976, 83
Tax savings
  calculation of, 203
  in re-syndication vs. new construction, 148
  in subsidized housing, 24
Tax shelter investing
  abusive shelters, 8, 10
  analyzing benefits of, 201-204, 209-210
  common misconceptions, 43-47
  comparing returns from, 197-210
  current economic climate, 3-8
  deduction-oriented shelters, 8

237

disposing of shelters, 25
due diligence, 32
  see also "Due diligence"
economic outlook, 219-223
exotic shelters, 9, 47
importance of economic value,
  25-28, 43, 46
investor suitability criteria, 13-17
rules for selection, 25, 33
shelters to avoid, 39-42
Tax underpayment penalties, 185,
191-194
  comparison of old and new
  rules, 192-194
Taxable gain
  calculation of, 87-88, 203-204
Thoroughbred horses
  breeding vs. racing, 171, 173

costs, 172
depreciation, 174, 175
syndication values for selected
  horses, 172, 173
tax shelter traps, 174-175

Underpayment penalties, see "Tax
underpayment penalties"

Venture Capital partnerships, see
"Research and development
partnerships"

Wildcat drilling, 63
Windfall Profit Tax, 3-5, 53, 54
  under ERTA, 187
Wrap-around mortgage, 44, 127